MARY M

D0671491

RECONCILED BEING
Love In Chaos

THE JOHN MAIN SEMINAR 1997

MEDIO MEDIA / ARTHUR JAMES

LONDON AND BERKHAMSTED

First published in Great Britain in 1997 by

MEDIO MEDIA LTD
in association with
ARTHUR JAMES LTD
70 Cross Oak Road Berkhamsted
Hertfordshire HP4 3HZ

A catalogue record for this book is available
from the British Library.

ISBN 0 85305 444 4

Permissions applied for

Cover & Page Design by StyloGraphics©
Email: StyloGraphics@Compuserve.com

Printed and Bound in Great Britain
by Guernsey Press Limited

Acknowledgements

The Organizing Committee of the John Main Seminar 1997 chaired by Msgr. Tom Fehily of Dun Laoghaire who warmly hosted the Seminar in true Irish fashion on behalf of The World Community for Christian Meditation at St. Patrick's College, Dublin.

Dom Laurence Freeman o.s.b. and the staff of the International Centre of The World Community who helped to produce this book.

My husband, Martin and children Emma, Justin and Sara Mai for their unstinting support and understanding in all my endeavours.

All this has been the work of God. He has reconciled us to himself through Christ and has enlisted us in this ministry of reconciliation.

St Paul's Second Letter to the Corinthians 5:18

Mary McAleese was born in Belfast in 1951. She graduated in law from Queen's University where she later became Pro-Vice-Chancellor. Her career has included a Chair at Trinity College Dublin and journalism. Her involvement in the struggle for peace in Northern Ireland has earned her world-wide recognition and respect. She is married with three children.

CONTENTS

INTRODUCTION

In Ireland we have a saying that there are no strangers here, just friends we have not met! Meditation is essentially a way of making new friends and renewing acquaintances. One such friend to many meditators, is the late Dom John Main. Twenty years ago he set off for Montreal to follow his vision of bringing meditative prayer into the mainstream of Christian experience not for its own sake but as an effective way of truly and profoundly experiencing the ever-presence of Christ in each of our lives. His early death did not end his role as Christian teacher or his mission. Both continue to grow, bringing the embrace of God's love to a wider and wider audience.

My own track record as a teacher of meditation is less than inspiring according to my daughter Emma. Some years ago when she was four or five I used to disappear into my study regularly for this mysterious thing called meditation. Asked to explain what I did there I simply told her I talked to God. One day she asked me if she could come too and would I teach her how to meditate.

Well, I thought John Main himself repeated like a mantra that meditation is simple. "Don't complicate it." he would say. "It's as easy as falling off a wall." Emma's bruised legs and missing front tooth were clear evidence that falling off walls was an area of considerable expertise. If Fr. John was right this should as they say North of the border be "wee buns". "Sit up straight." I told her, "Close your eyes lightly and repeat the word Maranatha over and over in absolute silence." I did the same. Five minutes into my meditation the little voice interrupted me. "Excuse me mammy, but is God talking to you?"

Ignoring everything John Main had ever said about meditation I rashly answered "Yes". "Right!" she said "Will you please tell him that when he is finished with you I am still waiting?"

And you are perhaps waiting and wondering where our time together in this book will lead us? Hopefully somewhere worthwhile across some of the issues of our own time and their relevance to the gospel; a journey into the relationship between belief and bullying, between faith and fury, between the gospel of love and the evil of sectarian and other forms of group hatred.

1

CHAOTIC HEARTS AND UNRECONCILED SOULS

For twelve years of my life I lectured in the Law School in Trinity College, Dublin, the same Law School which was home to John Main many years ago. One of Trinity's most endearing features is its quaint cobbled front square. In my early years the quaintness of the ancient cobble stones was largely nullified by the danger they posed to females in high heels. Racing to lunchtime Mass was a particularly fraught venture. More than once I am sure I scandalised visitors to the College by limping into the chapel audibly swearing at yet another sprained ankle. The cobble stones had become dipped and pitted by years of traffic. They were about as flat as the Alps and as treacherous. Then some genius decided to lift and level them. Each one was painstakingly removed and numbered so that it could be faithfully returned to its proper place. The job took months. When it was finished the flattened perfection was a marvel to behold. Within weeks however, the dips and valleys reappeared as if the ghosts of those who had passed that way were spending the nights clogdancing on the cobblestones. I took it as a cryptic reminder that while we appear to walk many paths for the first time, mostly we travel roads already well travelled, roads, for which there are guides, if only we have the wisdom to seek them and the humility to acknowledge and recognise them.

John Main was a couple of years dead before I discovered his tapes and writings though prayer has been a significant component of my life since child-hood. In seeking to mature in prayer I had stumbled my way into meditation and was surprised to find not only a fellow lawyer but one who had taught in the same law school and trodden the same cobblestones, but presumably in his case, not in high heels. The overlapping of lives was intriguing though not particularly unusual or remarkable. What was reassuring was to know that another career lawyer, a teacher like me, had lived a parallel inner life of the spirit which had ultimately become the focus of his entire being, relegating everything else to the margins.

Here was a man whose own life was replete with dips and valleys, highs and lows, as well as changes of direction. Like a heat seeking missile restlessly seeking out its target he ultimately found it, not in a place or institution but in his own inner being. And when he found it there was the joy of recognition and the surge of energy as his talents fused in the service of the mission he embarked on. It is the same journey to God we are all stumbling through one way or another.

John Main was very familiar with the landscape of my world. The sectarian chaos in Northern Ireland and the absence of reconciliation among Christians was part of his landscape also. What draws me to him and I am sure it is true of many people who have found him a trustworthy guide, is the fixedness of his focus, the refusal to be distracted from the agenda of being reconciled to God.

Reconciliation

My dictionary says simply that the word "reconcile" means "to make friends again". There is a presumption of a previous friendship, a closeness, which has been disturbed or ruptured by disagreement. These elements which are to be reconciled were previously known to each other and not only known, but they were once compatible friends. Reconciliation merely reestablishes the former order which prevailed. In conflicts as long and bitter as Northern Ireland's it is not easy to see where the previous friendship was or if it existed at all. For Christians, for anyone who believes in one God, a Creator of all humankind, the idea of a previous closeness has a very particular meaning. It describes our common ancestry in our common Creator, our bondedness to God as our Father/Mother and our bondedness to each other as brothers and sisters. The reconciliation at the heart of the Christian gospel is the full recognition of those bonds.

If we are not friends with each other, can we still be friends with God? "But," we may reply "I have lots of friends. We may have tiffs from time to time but we manage to stay friends nonetheless. I am not friendless and I love God. To whom then must I be reconciled?"

"I know my own and my own know me" [1]

Words of comfort or words to disturb? Words to quieten the chaos and wrap us up in love, reconciling us to God and to each other, or words of war to fuel hatred, to promote chaos, to see reconciliation as failure, obliteration of 'the other' as success? Have we chosen our friends too carefully, created an illusion of being people of love by selecting people whom it is easy to love?

Many years ago on my first day in a brief career as a junior barrister, I nervously entered a busy courtroom. I had all the unimportant paraphernalia, law degree, practising certificate, wig, gown, law books, I even had a client, God help him, but there were a couple of absolutely essential things missing. The first thing of paramount importance that I lacked was any idea of where I should sit. In Law School in those days they taught you how to parse and analyse decisions of the high appellate courts like the Supreme Court and the House of Lords, how to interpret the Constitution, how to interpret complex legislation but they didn't teach you where to sit in court on your first day. Even my client, a regular it seemed on the court circuit knew where he should sit. He threw himself into the public gallery with the air of a man who owned the place, but I, the advocate on whom he was relying to impress the court, hung awkwardly around the lawyers' benches in the hope that an obvious space would open up which I could claim. It didn't. The longer I stood the more I wished a black hole would open in the floor and swallow me. The second thing I lacked was the wit to ask someone to help me. Within minutes I no longer wanted my chosen vocation or my client all I wanted was my mammy. Everyone else seemed so confidently busy, so at home, so known. I would have settled for feeling invisible but actually I felt like a pair of Rosary beads in an Orange Lodge. Suddenly one of the busy lawyers looked up and caught my eye. Immediately he was at my side. Follow me he said. Sit beside me and I'll keep you right. He did. Gently and kindly he introduced me to everyone. They moved over on the bench and made space for one more. I now belonged. I was one of their own.

Anyone who has ever attended a conference will know that when you enter a room filled with people, many or all of them strangers, one of the great joys is to be already in the company of friends or to see a friend inside, someone you can purposefully walk towards and be welcomed by. We seek recognition and the comfort of the familiar. We know our own and they know us.

By contrast the person who is alone at the start of a meeting and who knows no-one, can feel awkward, isolated, a little uncomfortable just like me in that courtroom. Certainly over time, contact will be made and ice will be eventually broken, though I have often left conferences never having fully lost my sense of displacement and of awkwardness. But right at the start, the little groups of acquaintances and friends each one buzzing and chatting animatedly can seem like circles which are hermetically sealed. Only those who are known, who belong, can unlock the seal, provoke the welcoming words, and the embrace which draws a person into the group. For the person who has braved the event alone or who has not met up with a friend yet there is an inhibiting self-consciousness which may sit like an invisible barrier.

At the start of his powerful memoir 'An Evil Cradling', Brian Keenan, the Belfast born writer who was held hostage in Beirut for four years in the most appalling conditions by Islamic fundamentalists, says

"It is always hard to find a beginning"[2].

The cynic, observing the baleful sectarian violence in the place from which Keenan and I both come might add that finding an end is difficult too. The even more perceptive cynic might remark that difficult as it is to find a beginning or an end, finding a meaning is almost impossible. The most cynical commentator of them all P.J.O'Rourke says this is the

"Piece of Ireland that passeth all understanding!"[3]

Politicians from Ireland, Great Britain and Northern Ireland face the awesome task of achieving political reconciliation out of the chaos of conflicting ambitions, seething hatreds and deep-felt wounds. Intuitively we know that a cease-fire and a timetable for talks are only small pieces in a very irregularly shaped jigsaw because this squabble over the ownership of the large field that is Northern Ireland is of long duration. In 1922 Winston Churchill looking at a world emerging from the desecration of the Great War was able to say, wearily;

> *"great empires have been overturned..... The position of countries has been violently altered. The modes of thought of men, the whole outlook on affairs, the grouping of parties, all have encountered tremendous changes.... . But as the deluge subsides and the waters fall short we see the dreary steeples of Fermanagh and Tyrone emerging once again. The integrity of their quarrel is one of the few institutions that has been unaltered by the cataclysm."*[4]

Somehow though, the task of reconciling unionist and nationalist seems an almost manageable task by comparison with the task of reconciling the Catholic God with the Protestant God, the Allah of Islam with the God of Israel, the Hutu God with the Tutsi God, the Serbian God with the Croat God, the God of White racism with the God of Black Oppression. Politics might eventually lead to pragmatics and pragmatics to compromise, at least that is the hope. But Gods who compromise are in short supply globally. These Gods make powerful enemies as well as fiercely loyal friends. They know their own and their own know them. These Gods have favourites and their embrace is a curious thing- one arm is locked around those whom God favours, the other is held up as a barricade or a flailing weapon against those whom God abhors. Make no mistake about it these Gods hate, with an intensity so fierce it can combust into a Holocaust, a Rwanda, an ambush at Burntollet, a bomb at Enniskillen or Warrington, ethnic cleansing in Bosnia, a suicide bomber in a market square in Jerusalem, a teenage boy kicked to death because he is a Catholic, a woman raped because she is a Muslim, an English city centre bombed because it is British, or peaceful marchers shot in Derry by British troops because they are Irish.

One missionary in Rwanda is reported as saying- *"There are no devils left in hell. They are all in Rwanda."* But weren't the Tutsis Christian. Weren't the Hutus Christian too? Christian devils perhaps? Does the world know these Christians by their love? Where the name of Belfast is spoken is it to give praise for its love?

> *"I am the good shepherd; my sheep are known to me and know me; just as I am known to my father and know Him. And for these sheep I am laying down my life. I have other sheep too, which do not belong to this fold. I must bring them in too; they will listen to my voice so there will be one fold and one shepherd."*[5]

One fold and one shepherd. The impatient might ask, *"But when Lord, when!"*

Roots of Discord

Globally, what we see and experience is not oneness, one fold and one shepherd, but a diversity which is at times militant and aggressively exclusive. The natural gravitational pull of the group, the desire to belong which grabbed me on my first day in court, which affected that desire to be known and to be part of a family, a community, a nation, a culture, has its good healthy side but also its unredeemed, dark, leprous side.

Miroslav Wolf, the contemporary Croatian theologian says

> *"Group identities offer us homes in which to belong, spaces where we can be among our own and therefore be ourselves."*[6]

At the 1997 John Main Seminar in Dublin where I gave the talks which form this book we were one such group, at home with each other. A common interest in or curiosity about meditation had brought us together. I knew that I could talk freely there about God, faith, belief, inward journey, the spirit, prayer and a whole lot of other things without any sense of insecurity, embarrassment or tentativeness. The group had a shared language and a kind of shared identity which we did not necessarily share with our family or spouses or closest friends. I am more likely to discuss 16th century manure spreading practices with some of my family than meditation. Reading the many personal reminiscences about John Main by his friends and acquaintances I was struck by the number with whom he never raised the subject of meditation, never mind God. So the group with a common interest offers us a special kind of place and a special kind of friendly space as Wolf says. But he goes on to warn;

> *"The homes which group identities provide can be stifling, suppressing the difference and creativity of their non-conformist members. Bases of power can become fortresses into which we retreat, surrounding ourselves by impenetrable walls dividing 'us' from 'them'. In situations of conflict, they serve as encampments from which to undertake raids into enemy territory. Group identities are profoundly ambivalent: they are havens of belonging as*

well as repositories of aggression, suffocating enclosures as
well as bases of liberating power."[7]

In his poem "Clearances", Seamus Heaney describes an incident in the life of his great grand-mother. A Protestant by birth she had converted to Catholicism on marriage. On her way to Sunday Mass just after her marriage the chaos and exclusion into which her life had descended as a consequence of her changing sides is graphically described by the poet.

> *"A cobble thrown a hundred years ago*
> *Keeps coming at me, the first stone*
> *Aimed at a great-grandmother's turncoat brow.*
> *The pony jerks and the riot's on,*
> *She's crouched low in the trap,*
> *Running the gauntlet that first Sunday*
> *Down the Brae to Mass at a panicked gallop."*[8]

Were the stone-throwers devils? Were they strangers? Weren't they in fact former friends and family, people who had once loved this terrified girl but with a curiously conditional love offered only to fully paid up and subscribing members of the group? For the person who leaves or is expelled from the group not only is there a consequential loss of love but a vacuum filled rapidly by hate. Ireland, like many areas of conflict has a long history of similar incidents. No side has a monopoly on such stories though they may fantasise and claim that they have.

During a recent television programme on the systematic rape of women in Bosnia a shocked journalist asked how come the victims could so readily put names to those who had brutally defiled them. The answer was chilling.

> *"Because we went to school with them."*

The evidence is clear that deeply divided sectarian groups can live side by side, even in apparently integrated worlds but in reality each inhabits a parallel non-communicating universe.

In Helen Lewis's beautiful autobiography "A Time to Speak"[9] she writes of her ordeal in Auschwitz and the subsequent Long March which she barely survived. Her life's journey was eventually to take her to happier days, curiously enough in Belfast, where her talent as a choreographer was to grace that city for many decades. First though, the young Jewish dancer was consigned to the death-camps. Time and again the haunting beauty of her dancing so stirred the soul of the prison guards that she was passed over for selection for the gas chambers. It seems almost to defy belief that those who routinely sent millions to death could have enough refinement in their souls to respond to music and to dance. Yet they did and more than once it saved her life. On the Long March after Auschwitz, emaciated, diseased and tramping through snowdrifts with the retreating German Army it was her dearest friend also an Auschwitz inmate, the one whose support and love had kept her going through the worst of times, it was that friend who callously and deliberately left her to die. Perhaps deeper than all sectarian divisions and at the root of all human discord is the savagely isolated individual ego, ruthless in its determination to survive at all costs.

The shock of that betrayal was the most savage lesson of all. You might think that after Auschwitz Helen Lewis would have been beyond hurt, beyond all expectation of decency and humanity in another. But surprisingly there remained, forged in her heart, a clear belief in the resilience of love. From her captors she expected nothing less than brutality and when she found a glimmer of humanity it flooded her heart with hope. From her friend she expected love and fidelity, when she found it flawed, fragile and ultimately fallible, she almost died of despair. Brian Keenan makes a similar point that the brutality he experienced from his captors was infinitely more tolerable than the self-doubt and despair provoked by his own sense of worthlessness: the other face of the ego's proud arrogance.

In Beirut Brian Keenan and the other captives were mercilessly beaten and brutalised by men who loved God and loved their country. They had wives and families whom they loved. They had prayer lives as regular and disciplined as any contemplative monk. Keenan describes them as "Holy Warriors filled with righteous rage: all God-tormented and screaming Allah-u-Akbar" but as he says ominously, before we can self-righteously condemn his Muslim captors;

> "I who grew up in Belfast, perhaps knew the terrorist mind better than any other hostage. Knowledge was my sword. I could cut through our captor's aggression, their perversion, their constant humiliation. I could see the man, a man not defined by Islam or by ethnic background. a man more confused than the man in chains, a man more hurt and anguished than the man he had just beaten." [10]

Its a bizarre but embarrassingly familiar image-the captor kicking the captive in the name of God and the captive in his pain shouting "Why me Lord." Belfast or Beirut it is all the same. Living in Belfast and increasingly out of synch with the ethnic group into which he was born, Keenan had grown angry and frustrated with his homeplace and the way it cornered a person, straitjacketed him, refusing to give him space to grow, or to change. Feeling trapped he thought he would find freedom in Beirut. Instead as he said himself he simply confronted the same "entrapment in another place." The roots of division cannot after all be completely explained or solved by politics or history.

Keenan's 'reconciliation' came, not on the day his captors set him free but rather when over the course of four long years in the company of his fellow captors, all from diverse backgrounds, he attempted to find meaning and wholeness in his experience. What he discovered is immensely important because he discovered it from first principles. Brian Keenan did not set out for Beirut on a spiritual journey. He did not seek through a life of prayer to come to a greater knowledge of God and he did not emerge from captivity shouting "I have found God, I am born again." (His great sense of humour alone testified to that. He was a welcome antidote to the familiar baleful phenomenon of those who find God and lose their sense of humour simultaneously!) But this is what he did say-

> "We had each turned inward intensely. In searching through the complex panorama of our past one thing emerged again and again our relationship to and understanding and experience of love underlay everything else... John (his fellow captive John McCarthy) and I found great solace in reading the Psalms. The anguished suffering mind that created them and had cried out to God in his suffering reflected much of our own condition. Exhausted with profound questions and never finding an answer, we took relief in devotional moments. It seemed we could meditate on the active nature and qualities of what this God of love could mean in human terms... At times God seemed so real and so intimately close. We talked not of a God in the Christian tradition but of some force more primitive, more immediate and more vital, a presence rather than a set of beliefs... In its own way our isolation had expanded the heart not to reach out to a detached God but to find and become part of whatever God may be..."[11]

From Conflict to the Cloud of Unknowing

Brian Keenan's discovery is the same discovery made by John Cassian, by Theresa of Avila, Catherine of Sienna, Julian of Norwich, Thomas Merton, Teilhard de Chardin, Bede Griffiths and John Main among many more. Talking to God or about God is a poor and imperfect substitute for experiencing the presence of God. Once you have broken through the barrier of an immature, sensational and superficial relationship with God and have come into the knowledge of a love so blindingly real and illuminating , all previous descriptions of God, all boxes to which he has been consigned become redundant. You have indeed passed through the "cloud of unknowing" to a more real world beyond the delusions of the ego's pride or sectarian hatred.

One of the reasons why I draw on Brian Keenan's story is that having carried on his back the chaos of a fragmented sectarian homeland in Belfast and the baggage of a fractured sectarian adopted homeland in Lebanon, he ultimately reconciles their respective conflicting Gods in his belief in the triumph of love. These small, mean petty Gods are small, petty men dressed up in what they imagine is God's clothing but even in their meanness and smallness the God of all envelops them in meaning and in love.

Keenan's is no mawkish sentiment, no denominational advocacy. Wary, he even shies away from the name 'God'. His path to reconciliation of a sort lay in brute, crass, vulgar, tunneling in the small cramped miserable space of the imprisoned self, with no guru for guidance, with only the clumsiest of tools, digging down through layer after layer of cultural silt, spiritual sediment, and emotional compost, to an experience of love which allowed him to dwell fully humanly, inside that iniquitous physical space. No matter how depraved the conditions in his cell he managed to make it among other things, an altar, a sacred place. How? Because he occupied it and he was loved unconditionally and he had come to know that awesome truth. He clawed his way to a real redemption not just for himself but for his captors. Their God was made redundant, vanquished. Their God was a God of Judgment and of vengeance, a God they feared. As he says;

> "Their submission to God was an act of repression."[12]

Keenan's acknowledgment of and submission to love was by contrast a liberation. The jailer and the jailed. Which was really which? As Keenan says;

> "These men existed in their own kind of prison, perhaps more confining than the one that held us."[13]

When Brian Keenan emerged from his captivity, Northern Ireland was still in chaos, still only halfheartedly seeking elusive reconciliation, still fighting its bitter fight. The Lebanon was still in ruins. Not a lot had changed externally. He had changed though, changed irrevocably emerging so deeply reconciled to his own being that those of us who listened to him and read him, envied him his insight and saw about him the aura of one who has passed successfully through the "cloud of unknowing."

Physically chained to another human being as he and John McCarthy had been, there had been no room for pretence or guises of any sort. They saw each other in ways which were raw and comprehensively lacking in privacy to an extent that even the closest of marriages could never achieve and indeed might never want to achieve. Not everyone and not every relationship could survive the scale of intrusiveness that these men endured.

Crucial to the extraordinary journey they travelled in that tiny room was their willingness to change, to accept the damaging baggage that each carried, to strip it away and to accept with joy the differences between them and with respect, the common humanity they shared.

> *"In the circumstances in which we found ourselves physically chained together we both realised an extraordinary capacity to unchain ourselves from what we had known and been- to set free those trapped people and parts of ourselves. We came to understand that these trapped people included our own captors and we were able to incorporate them into our healing process."* [14]

So what does any of this mean for us? What are we to take from it?

It raises inevitably the question of our own baggage and the extent to which we have insight about it and the extent to which it gets in the way of travelling our own journey through the "cloud of unknowing".

It raises the question too of how important is one woman's or one man's journey? How much impact in the scale of things will one man or woman's change of heart or conviction have? Is the problem so vast, so intractable that one person's heart turning afresh to God makes no difference? Social reconciliation must be based on the individual's readiness to change, to be reconciled to his or her own particular universe? Can that one person make a difference to society? The evidence points to a definite 'yes'.

The story of the late John Main himself helps to illustrate this. As a young civil servant in Malaya he chanced to meet Swami Satyananda. That encounter introduced him to meditation but it also introduced him to a novel way of looking at God. The Swami was of course Hindu, the young Main, Christian. *"Will you teach me to meditate?"* the young Christian asked the older Hindu monk.

What followed was an unlikely encounter which is worth dwelling on. In it we can see the green shoots of hope that the strongest differences between people, even the deepest divisions are contained in a single all-embracing reality. That reality is the source of reconciliation and healing for individuals and societies alike. We can see here perhaps, the evidence, that there is, despite our best efforts to mask it, one fold and one shepherd.

The Swami did not say to the young Christian monk-

"I only teach those of the Hindu faith."

or

" I will only teach you if you embrace the Hindu faith."

or

" I will only teach you the Hindu way."

or

"As a non-Hindu you are not allowed into my temple."

Any or all of those responses would have been open to him and would have sounded familiar to someone from the Christian tradition. Instead he accepted John Main's Christianity not as a problem he would have to overcome, but as a discipleship he wanted to honour and to enrich. He would help John Main grow in knowledge of the single all-embracing Reality. Why? Because ultimately Swami Satyananda was secure in his knowledge of God. Ultimately he knew that everyone who seeks God's real presence, no matter by what route, or under what label, adds to the sum total of love in a world thirsting and hungering for love. By sharing his understanding of God with another of a different faith, the swami was not contaminating it, nor diluting it. Quite the opposite! He was enriching it in a way which defies mathematical computation. He was not betraying any sacred tradition but honouring an old one, as old as humanity itself, recognising a brother in God and welcoming him in love and without fear.

Love is Indivisible

The poet Shelley puts it this way –

> *"True love in this differs from gold and clay, that to divide is not to take away. "*[15]

The nearest I have come to a comprehension of the mathematical mystery that is God's love is in a story that comes from my experience as a mother. When my first daughter Emma was born, I approached the new role of motherhood with the jaundiced eye of older sister to five brothers and three sisters. I had had babies up to my tonsils throughout my teenage life. My mother and her siblings had taken to heart the gospel call to increase multiply and fill the earth, except that they thought they had to do it singlehandedly. Between them they had sixty children most of them younger than me. If the truth be told I had a relatively underwhelmed attitude to babies generally. I was surprised therefore to find myself so completely overwhelmed and totally smitten by my own daughter. I loved her to bits. Consequently when I discovered some two years later that I was expecting twins I hit an unexpected crisis. These twins were badly wanted but for nine awful months I struggled to comprehend how I was going to divide this wonderful river of love for Emma between two more children. I was heartbroken for her. She was now to have two thirds of her normal allotment of love withdrawn and distributed among her rival siblings. I thought it a shameful thing to do to a child, but what else was there to do?

How little I knew. When the twins were born and I passed through that knowledge and experience barrier that books are incapable of explaining I knew how rudimentary, simplistic and pathetic was my comprehension of love. There was no need to share what Emma had. Here were two new babies, each one with their unique river of grace and love. Not only did I not have to share Emma's love, it was now enhanced and even more vibrant, touched as it was by these two new lives.

You cannot divide love. Its nature is to multiply, to embrace openly and widely, to draw in, not to exclude, to make each feel part of the group, to make each feel completely at home, to reconcile.

Exclusivity is not in the nature of God. He made each one of us, called us by our name, knew us before we were born, has the very hairs on each head counted. God has no favourites. Captor and captive are his cherished children. Calvary is his gift to all. The Resurrection is his promise. The Second Coming is his invitation. It is an invitation to experience his loving presence, to share it and to bring the world out of chaos into reconciliation with Him.

Perfect environments in which to seek that loving presence are hard to find. Our environment in Northern Ireland with its sectarian hatred, its savage murders, even with a cease-fire, its verbal violence, its strutting machismo, this is where we who live there, have to pitch our tent and start the journey to centred calmness and reconciliation. There is no guarantee that anyplace else is better (as Brian Keenan found out to his cost).

If there is not much that is edifying from time to time in the place we inhabit it is worth recollecting that there was nothing much edifying about the circumstances of Christ's capture and death. The Northern Presbyterian poet W.R. Rodgers captured it brilliantly in his poem "Resurrection".

> "This was a rough death, there was nothing tidy about it,
> No sweetness, nothing noble.
> Everything stuck out awkwardly and angular...
> Still that is how things always happen, lousily,
> But later on, the heart edits them out lovingly,
> Abstracts the jeers and jags, imports a plan
> Into the pain, and calls it history.
> We always go back to gloss over some roughness,
> To make the past happen properly as we want it to happen.
> But this was a hard death..."[16]

As Christians looking at the Cross two thousand years down the road it is easy to see ourselves as sympathetic and heartbroken, innocent spectators at Christ's death. Before asking what if any role we might play in the hatreds and fractures and fissures in our own country and communities perhaps we might ask had we been Romans in Jerusalem 2000 years ago where would we have been on Good Friday and doing what? Had we been Islamic fundamentalists in Beirut in 1986, had we been German prison guards in 1944, where would we have been and doing what?

Each of our lives is lived out in some place, with its own history and its own context. The complexity of that context, the intractable nature of its hurts and hates may make us feel helpless but wherever that place may be and however long our stay in it, it is in some sense our own Gethsemani. It is the place and the time, when we have been scheduled to watch and pray with Christ. To wait, watch and pray can be a work of reconciliation as well as acting, doing, marching or speaking out. Each place has its own chaos, its own fractures and fault lines, its own unreconciled balance sheet. It also has a chorus of voices of those who still hope that there is truth, that there can be justice, that there will be peace. Christians should have no difficulty identifying the source of that hope. As

Leonardo Boff says

> "As attested to by all the cultures and civilizations the
> world has known there is a principle of hope at work
> wherever pole have lived that generates great excitement
> and utopian visions in spite of the fact that of the 3400
> years of recorded human history 3166 were years of war and
> the remaining 234 were years of preparing for war."[17]

So many human hearts have lived and died in the chaos fuelled
by hate. In our era, the era of liberation movements all over the
world, the fuel of hope has been the possibility of change, leading to
changed hearts, changed souls, changed politics and changed
practices.

Christ's mission in relation to the salvation of Creation is, we
have to believe, still unfolding. We are playing a role whether
holding it back or nudging it forward. To the extent that we keep
watch through the long nights of the soul that are our own personal
Gethsemani and keep our focus on Christ, we are changed. The
watching and waiting with Christ, the sharing in his suffering, these
things change us as individuals. Without change there is no growth.
In the three years of his public ministry Christ convulsed and
transformed the lives of his apostles. They changed so much that as
they emerged from the terror of their self-imposed imprisonment in
the Upper Room they might have said the words that Brian Keenan
cryptically remarked to the taxi driver on his final journey to
freedom through Syria to Ireland.

"So, this is the road to Damascus!"[18]

FOOTNOTES CHAPTER 1.

1   John 10: 14
2   "An Evil Cradling" by Brian Keenan pub. Hutchinson,
    London 1992
3   "Holidays in Hell" by P.J.O'Rourke pub. Picador 1989
4   Winston Churchill 1922
5   John 10: 14-17
6   "A Vision of Embrace Theological Perspectives on Cultural
    Identity and Conflict" by Miroslav Wolf, Fuller Theological
    Seminary, Pasadena, California
7   ibid.
8   "Clearances" from "The Haw Lantern" by Seamus Reancy
    pub. Faber and Faber 1987
9   "A Time to Speak" by Helen Lewis
10 Brian Keenan, op.cit.
11 ibid.
12 ibid.
13 ibid.
14 ibid.
15 "Epipsychidion" by Percy Bysshe Shelley
16 "Resurrection" from "Poems" by W.R. Rodgers pub.
    Gallery Books 1993
17 "Teologica del cautivero y de la liberacion", by Leonardo Boff
    pub. Madrid Ediciones Paulinas 1978
18 Brian Keenan, op.cit.

2

LEARNING HOW TO UNLEARN

"You have heard that it was said, Thou shalt love thy neighbour and hate thy enemy. But I tell you, Love your enemies, do good to those who hate you, pray for those who persecute and insult you, that so you may be true children of your father in heaven, who makes his sun rise on the evil and equally on the good, his rain fall on the just and equally on the unjust."[1]

We believe Jesus came to change the world, radically, root and branch, for all time. His preaching life was dedicated to changing how people thought and how they acted. Before they changed they had to challenge and be challenged on all those things they had previously believed and held dear. He came to give them life and life in abundance, flowing from this new way of seeing things. One of the dynamics at the heart of that new life was the *wholeness* of it, the mysterious way it reconciled body and soul, neighbour and neighbour, self to self and self to God. Those who embraced and who embrace fully the new life know that to be imprisoned in knowledge long past its sell-by date is to be only partly alive.

Have we learnt how to unlearn? If we put our own beliefs, assumptions, values, prejudices under a critical spotlight would they pass the fresh smell test. Do they have the odour of sanctity or of sanctimony?

In 1991 Archbishop Robin Eames head of the Church of Ireland and Cardinal Cathal Daly, Roman Catholic Primate of All Ireland, acting on behalf of the Inter Church Meeting invited me along with a Quaker colleague John Lampen, to co-chair a working party on the subject of sectarianism in Ireland and the churches' response to it.

We assembled a team of seventeen men and women, lay and clerical, of virtually all Christian denominations in Northern Ireland to undertake the task and we set about it with enthusiasm. All of us had been involved in ecumenical discussion over many years and some of us were long-standing friends who had never uttered a cross word to one another. We were all genuinely concerned about the awful crucifixion that sectarian hatred was hammering into our country. We set out enthusiastically to cook up an agreed ecclesiastical recipe for the elimination of sectarianism, a spiritual potion or vaccine which we the good guys could administer to the bad guys who presumably would form a line outside our churches like starving people queuing for food and penicillin at relief camps.

We agreed on a working definition. That seemed a good and auspicious start.

> *"Sectarianism is a complex of attitudes, beliefs, behaviours and structures in which religion is a significant component and which directly or indirectly infringes the rights of individuals or groups and/or influences or causes situations of destructive conflict."*[2]

It was a particularly good definition for it focused on consequences rather than attitudes or intentions. It allowed for sectarian consequences to flow from acts committed by those who saw themselves as pure of heart. Unfortunately we had not reckoned on providing ourselves with first-hand evidence of sectarianism thus defined, from our own conduct!

We were to learn painfully the truth of Miroslav Wolf's words.

> *"The practice of exclusion is not just something that the evil and barbaric others out there do; exclusion is also what we, the good and civilised people right here do... the tendency lurks in the dark regions of all our hearts, seeking an opportunity to find a victim."*[3]

By a curious twist of fate all of us, Catholic and Protestant members of the Working Party chose the same victim. At one juncture it seemed that our common victim was the only thing we were destined to agree on. An American Mennonite, one of our group in an unguarded moment had agreed to write a paper on the history of sectarianism in Ireland. He seemed a sensible choice. He was not going to write an Irish Catholic nationalist version nor a British Protestant Unionist version. In the event that was the problem. He wrote a paper that provoked spontaneous combustion in everyone. For months up until we discussed his paper, when we met and talked our attitudes and discussions were monuments to civility. After all that nasty sectarianism was *out there. We* were all Christians, decent people. No sectarian idea could enter our heads!

On the day that Joe Leichty's paper was read and discussed, the group members heaped abuse on each other and on him so spontaneously, so unguardedly that I was certain there would either be seventeen minority reports or no report at all. Joe went back to Maynooth on the train, happy to have escaped with his life but otherwise in shock. Where had the civility gone? Like all facades built on weak foundations it had collapsed under pressure. We had codded each other, deluded each other, brought to the table not our honesty and our trust that we would be loved no matter how honest we were, but our practiced dissembling, our fear of angry rejection, our craven pretence described so deftly by Seamus Heaney in his poem "Whatever You Say Say Nothing". (Heaney's reference in the poem to the "wee six" is a colloquialism for the six counties of Ireland which comprise the state of Northern Ireland.)

"................. *The famous*
Northern reticence, the tight gag of place
And times: Of the 'wee six' I sing
Where to be saved you only must save face
And whatever you say, you say nothing.

Smoke-signals are loudmouthed compared with us:

> *O land of password, handgrip, wink and nod,*
> *Of open minds as open as a trap,*
> *Where tongues lie coiled, as under flames lie wicks..."*[4]

That day was a Damascus day. We saw with embarrassing clarity how much hidden baggage we had carried into those meetings. We learnt the lesson that is so important in conflict based societies, that festering silence is unhealthy, because each side believes itself rightly or wrongly to be the victim of the other. Each must have its say, must speak out its pain and must be listened to in respectful silence. We must learn the skill of really listening even when every word burns. There is a time to speak out and a time to be silent. Not until all the hurts are out, without being shouted down, can real healing and reconciliation begin. The embrace of God's love does not demand of us that we suppress our hurts actual or perceived. Quite the opposite, but others have hurts too. Miroslav Wolf says we must

> *"make space for the other in the self and rearrange the self*
> *in the light of the other's presence."*[5]

This concept of a reconciling embrace is based on telling our truth, and seeking justice. It is one which insists that truth be told, that injustice be named and both sides have their say. It is not afraid of facing these things or of testing their validity, because it confronts them not with anger and vengeance but with forgiveness and love and in the knowledge that solid foundations for lasting peace cannot be built on a false repressive silence. The South African Truth and Reconciliation Commission comes to mind as a model which fits this embrace. Confronting our mistakes, our baggage, our muddled thoughts and hurtful deeds is about unlearning; it is the hard rite of passage to spiritual peace. In the case of the Working Party on sectarianism we were so horrified by our public vehemence, that a contriteness and humility descended on our labours like tongues of fire in the Upper Room. We finished our work but for most of us the journey into self-knowledge and self-reconciliation had only just begun.

Women Speaking Truth

At the end of Chapter One Brian Keenan was travelling the road to Damascus and to freedom of a sort. The body he brought home was the same body but the heart and soul had been emptied of so much and replenished with so much that it is no exaggeration to say he had undergone a process of conversion, a convulsive process of learning and just as important, of unlearning. He was not of course the first to travel that road that famous road to Damascus. By far its most important traveller in the history of Christendom was St. Paul. Now St. Paul is a saint about whom I confess to a measure of ambivalence and from time to time we have had our differences of opinion, not least on the subject of women.

This incident which involves an encounter with Saint Paul has a bearing on the subject of reconciliation and the importance of unlearning our prejudices.

Twelve or thirteen years ago I was asked to preach in a Cathedral. I was a to be the first woman to mount that forbidding pulpit who did not have a yellow duster and a tin of Mr. Sheen furniture polish in her hand. I had said 'yes' in circumstances not unlike the circumstances which brought me to give the John Main Seminar. I was flattered to be asked to speak but also nervous. My instincts told me it was doubtful if I had anything original or worthwhile to say. In the end it came right down to the fact that I lacked the humility to say no.

The night before my appearance in the Cathedral, I was experiencing real difficulty in thinking of something significant to commit to the very blank and very reproachful sheet of paper in front of me. In desperation I turned to prayer. "Look Lord." I said

"I could be doing with a bit of help here. After all I am appearing in one of your branch offices tomorrow so the least you could do is point me towards something vaguely engaging to say. It doesn't have to be earthshatteringly original, after all I want my talk to have something in common with every other talk from the same pulpit; just less than totally inane and boring would be a big improvement on the norm. I lifted down my New Testament having waited a few minutes for the message to be received and understood even by a male God. The book fell open at that part of St. Paul's first letter to the Corinthians so familiar to all women and to far too many men, chapter 14 verses 34 to 36

> "Women are to be silent in church. They are not permitted
> to speak... That a woman should make her voice heard in
> the church is not seemly."

Needless to remark I was inclined to find the Lord's intervention less than helpful in the circumstances. An old adage of my mother's came to mind – sometimes the worst things that can happen is that the Lord answers your prayers!

However reflecting on that encounter again as I have done many times, I decided

1. that the Lord has a very, very mischievous sense of humour
2. that if St. Paul accompanies him at the second coming he is being marched straight down to the Equal Opportunities Commission to give and account of himself.
3. taking a generous and maybe even intriguing interpretation of St. Paul's words – could they be the first biblical evidence of a new commandment given specially to women – seek the silence, go meditate? (I doubt it!)

I finally concluded however that the central message which I believe the Lord was drawing my attention to was and remains the fact that St. Paul dominates 2000 years of Christendom as the man who most famously, most dramatically changed his mind. From being a tormentor of Christians he became their most powerful, most persuasive advocate. Once a brutish captor he voluntarily became the captive. Everything he had once believed became anathema to him. He shed it as a snake sheds its old skin. Saul became Paul, a new name, a new identity, same body, same eyes, refurbished soul, refurbished heart, refurbished mind and ultimately a new life-destination. But even the new Paul was capable of old flawed thinking. Even a refurbished mind has its cobwebs.

Aspects of the life of John Main come to mind. He was a man of many names and many dramatic, courageous changes. For courage is an essential component of change, particularly change which sets you at odds with your group, family, identity, culture, denomination or nation. Known to his family as Douglas, the man we know as John Main, used another of his baptismal names, Victor when he joined the Canons Lateran as a young man. His time with them in Rome in 1949/50 was not happy and there is evidence that he battled intellectually, spiritually and emotionally but privately for a long time before finally deciding to leave. Paul Harris's book of recollections "John Main by Those Who Knew Him" contains an article by the Dominican priest Father Paul Bowe who knew John Main during those early days in Rome. His insight into the things which Main found difficult to live with, shows that Main had an astute insight of remarkable maturity and sensitivity, well ahead of his time.

Father Bowe remarks that some biographies of John Main found the reasons for his departure from the Canons Lateran mysterious;

> " What I have to say may only add to the mystery; but at the time it was no mystery to me, at any rate.
>
> Sometime towards the end of the academic year in 1950 he called in to see me at San Clemente... To my great surprise he was not his usual good-humoured, sensible, balanced self. On the contrary he was very agitated and disturbed; there was no sign whatsoever of is sense of humour, or even

*of ordinary indignation. In fact his whole demeanour was
quite out of character. He went on to tell me that he was
thinking of pulling out altogether... it emerged that he was
desperately upset about the atmosphere of the international
house of studies in which he was living... Apparently to use
a modern term it was anti-feminist; in fact as far as the
priests were concerned, it was quite simply anti-woman.
According to John, 'women' were as far as priests were
concerned, to be regarded as 'snares of the devil'. Given half
a chance they would lead us, seminarians and priests astray
from our vocations... John had his wartime experiences
behind him and the maturity that goes with them, so one
can imagine the effect the kind of tommyrot he was being
exposed to was having on him. The strange thing about the
whole business was that he had never mentioned anything
like that to me before, even though we used to meet nearly
every day. I could only conclude afterwards that it must
have been festering away like a boil that needed to be
lanced but never was."[6]*

The issue of church-related/religious attitudes to women is
relevant in our reflection on reconciliation because there are some
inescapable and disturbing parallel's with political and denominational sectarianism. Ultimately all forms of exclusion and
exclusivity are based on what Miroslav Wolf calls a "logic of purity...
a logic which reduces, ejects and segregates"[7]

Not all exclusion is as crass or violent as ethnic cleansing. It has
its subtler modes. One of them is even apparently generous. Become
like us, it says and you can have a life. Become British, become Irish
surrender your identity, adopt mine and the conflict is solved. Even
more subtle is the exclusion which patronises – if you are a good
coloured boy or a good little girl we will let you work at this job or
live in this neighbourhood. We are the decision-makers and we tell
you what you are and what you may become.

Each form of exclusion opens up in a community and in the

hearts of individuals the fractures and fissures which characterise dysfunctional societies, dysfunctional people and dysfunctional relationships. They create anxieties which at once make stillness difficult because they provoke conflict and yet at the same time challenge us to make stillness and reconciliation possible. We have to make sense of the gospel in this world, as it is, because we do not have any other.

Two Forms of Marginality

Let me describe the pincer movement in which the warp and weft of my own life came to be shaped, some might say distorted by growing up in a world where to be a woman and a Catholic was to some extent at least, to be doubly excluded and marginalised if not doubly deviant!

I was born in Belfast between the Passionist monastery and the Orange Hall. In the former God was male, the altar was a male preserve, priests were heroes, and every mother wanted a son a hero. 'My son the priest' had a cachet which even 'my daughter the nun' could not hope to emulate. It was understood. God was male Father, male Son and male Holy Spirit. He was also by a happy coincidence Roman Catholic and probably Irish his parents presumably having emigrated from Ireland to heaven during the Famine! The Catholic God had long since abandoned his 16th century teaching that outside Catholic walls there could be no salvation, but presumably since this was in the days before e-mail and faxes, the message had not quite reached all corners of his Church. Rather grudgingly this God conceded that Protestants could be saved but it was generally understood this was in spite of their churches and not because of them. From the Orange Hall came another image of God, God the protector of Protestants, who had ordained that the Northwest corner of Northern Ireland would be Protestant and British. in perpetuity, beginning 1921. This God believed the Pope was an

anti-Christ, a deadly enemy and a man of sin. This God, to borrow
an inelegant phrase used by one well known Northern Christian
minister, believed Catholic women were "incubators for the
papacy", and all Catholics were in error. These Gods carried their
crosses like lances in a jousting tournament. Gods of appallingly
narrow perspective and parochial obsessiveness. Fidgety Gods who
brooded over small bits of the world with a warm embrace only for
the chosen few and not the wide embrace of the God I came to know
and need.

In the monastery there were over forty men who, dressed in their
flowing black habits, dominated the thinking and spiritual
landscape of my childhood. I was taken aback to hear my daughter
ask me some years ago if monks were examples of cross-dressers!
Strange how a new vocabulary can shake your perspective! I owe
those prayerful men a lot for their love of God was palpable but
there was also a deficit. It was not deliberate or malintended but
there was a deficit nonetheless. On the day I spoke out loud my
desire to be a lawyer, the first to say 'You can't because you are a
woman; you can't because no-one belonging to you is in the law',
was the Dublin born parish priest who weekly shared a whiskey or
three with my father. It was said with the kind of dismissive
authority which is intended to silence protest or debate. The owner
of superior knowledge, of real certitude had spoken and that was
that. The same priest incidentally kept a double-entry scoreboard of
the indignities heaped on Catholics by the Protestant Government
at Stormont many of which ironically involved keeping Catholics
out of jobs for no reason other than the fact that they were
Catholics. The irony of the similar group exclusion of women was
unfortunately lost on him. My mother had inculcated into us a
respect for the priesthood bordering on awe. I watched therefore in
amazement as the chair was pulled out from under the cleric and he
was propelled to the front door before the bottle of baby Powers had
been uncorked. "You – out" she roared at him "And you" she said
to me "ignore him!" That was the only advice I ever received from

either parent on the subject of career choice.

My schooling was all in convent schools so it would be untrue to say that there were no role models of working women for me. Between the nuns and my mother's own sisters there were many but there were also demarcation lines so clear, so defined that even now decades later, the same mother who so ably dispatched the sexist priest is able rather lamely to say, "I don't support women priests but I don't know why." I am saddened by the first part of her sentence but heartened by the second. If she knew why she opposed women priests I would really be worried! Those same demarcation lines on one side of which was authority and the other deference also allowed me many years later when the subject of women and priesthood was broached to say equally lamely, I do not understand the exclusion of women from the priesthood but then I am not a theologian. The historic parallels with the reasons why women could not be lawyers, could not be admitted to universities, could not be admitted to vote, had to surrender careers on marriage, did not escape me, I simply buried them. To challenge the awesome authority of the hierarchy seemed to open up an aptly named Pandora's box of things which might be difficult to swallow. If the Church was wrong, on an issue on which it spoke with a chilling clarity and certainty, then how many other errors might lie buried in that theology. There was a comfort in burying myself inside the group consciousness and putting my hands over my ears so that I could not hear the doubts that were running about in my head. To pit myself against the group meant challenging, mother, father, family, parish, community and to live with some form of exclusion which, whether mild rebuke or subtle shunning, would inevitably follow.

The Dominican nuns to whom I owe my happy secondary education taught me about that great philosophical Colossus, St. Thomas Aquinas. Unfortunately they did not teach me *all* about him. It was twenty years later that I discovered that I had been introduced to edited highlights only. Had I read what t he had to say in the Summa Theologica about the inferiority of women,[8] I might have begun to understand the connections through time, teaching and cultures which have shaped and circumscribed the roles permitted to women. But, before I knew, it was easier to feign ignorance than to face the doubt. The seed of doubt was planted nonetheless because one simple observation about truth is that it pointblank refuses to go away. It always finds a crevice to bubble through. It worries the minutest space until it pushes through to the light. As John Main and Thomas Merton both experienced, if the growth of the seed is suppressed, it festers until it eventually needs radical treatment.

In the political landscape of Northern Ireland separate identities and ambitions are shored up by conflicting versions of history, conflicting political ambitions and conflicting religious beliefs. Two separate sets of knowledge wrap people up, hermetically sealing them into systems of certainties and beliefs which resist contamination by doubt or updating. Inside one package resides all that is right and good. Inside the other resides all that is wrong and bad. The problem is of course that even if you and I occupy opposite packages we both believe we are in the one which monopolizes good and righteousness. Worse still our separate histories have taught us not only what to think but also crucially and much more intractably, how to think. What is true of the political landscape is if not exactly replicated at least mirrored in the sphere of gender and church and indeed in many spheres where relationships have broken down in a mire of mutual recrimination. The indicators are familiar – conflicting versions of the gospel, clashing theologies, claim and counterclaim, accusations of sedition, of grave error, of powerseeking, of lack of humility, of arrogance, threats of excommunication, accusations of fallibility and claims of infallibility. God is on my side says one. God is on mine says the other. The air is thick with the politics and the practice of exclusion.

And while the shouting match is going on, as each side rubbishes the other, what spiritual energy are we wasting, what richness are we denying to our world? What really would happen if both traditions in the North and both genders in the Church embraced each other in a God-trusting compassion which abandons the need for definitive victories and definitive doctrines? Is it possible as Merton believed that only when you abandon the self do you abandon fear? We already know the dismal balance sheet of the gospel of exclusion. What of the balance sheet we have not yet seen but have had meagre yet exhilarating glimpses of, the balance sheet of the gospel of embrace?

Dr. Anthony Padovano, who writes so powerfully on Merton says

"It is foolish for any culture to assume it is not profoundly influenced by a myth system. Such a denial is a myth itself."[8]

The Northern Irish poet Tom Paulin born into the Protestant community and culture describes his upbringing as puritan and anti-aesthetic. He was, he says, taught to be suspicious of what is rhetorical or ornate.

I by contrast, raised in the same country but in the Roman Catholic tradition, was nurtured in the rhetoric of the doctrine of transubstantiation, the smell of incense, the plaster statues, and apparitions, the very things Paulin was taught to be suspicious of. I grew up comfortable with them. He grew up uncomfortable with them. Already from early childhood in our two worlds we were learning to view each other not as interestingly different but as suspiciously, dangerously, different. We learnt early that we had nothing to learn from each other or to offer each other.

My mother grew up in a world where women left school young, married, gave up work and had nine children. The altar was her comfort in despair, the priest her ally in handing on the faith. Priests were men. Altar servers were boys. Feminism – what was that? "Equal opportunities" might just as well have been a new television game show.

I grew up part of the new brash generations which flooded the professions when free third level education became a (now rapidly disappearing) reality. Seamus Heaney describes these generations in his poem "From the Canton of Expectation" as having

"intelligences, brightened and unmannerly as crowbars."[9]

The metaphor of crowbar is particularly apt. A lot of very heavy stones needed to be removed from the mouth of the tombs which they had sealed! We learnt the language of equality, of human rights, of gender consciousness, a language which separated us from our parents and our teachers generation. We were still learning long after we had left their care and we were unlearning fast. The language of the church had to run to catch up with us. The excitement of our new language exhilarated us. As old ways fell, and new people became included, as old ideologies toppled and new alliances formed we could feel the earth moving to the pulse of what we believed was the grace of the Holy Spirit moving through its once clogged arteries. But amidst the hope of this new dawn there was a great and sad disappointment. Just as Tom Paulin's world and mine were suspicious of each other and uncomfortable with each other so too within my own faith system, two groups were forming, the 'conservatives' and the 'progressives', and their contemptuous rhetoric similarly based on mutual incomprehensibility.

If ever a cloud of unknowing hung thick about a church this cloud over unreconciled gender issues is it. We have heard the calls to battle, to winning and to losing but remarkably not to prayer. I have sometimes been guilty of losing sight of love too often in the passion of debate, and of too readily indulging in the language of "ya boo we're winning", or in the puerile and ultimately sterile my God- is- bigger- than -your- God style of dialogue.

Pope Paul VI asserted in 1975 that "the most pressing need at the moment is advancing the cause of women at every level both in society and in the church."[10] Twenty years later Pope John Paul was able to say "In every time and place our conditioning has been an obstacle to the progress of women. Women's dignity has often been unacknowledged, they have often been relegated to the margins of society and even reduced to servitude... If objective blame especially in particular contexts has belonged to not just a few members of the Church for this I am truly sorry."

The words of Pope Paul VI in 1976 are still heartening and hopeful after many years of struggle;

> "It is evident that women are meant to form part of the living and working structure of Christianity in so prominent a manner that perhaps not all their potentialities have yet been made clear."[11]

Yet as the theologian Fr. Dermot Lane has written;

> "There is a serious credibility gap between the theory and practice of the Catholic Church in regard to women... the Church has not followed up its statements with actions... Indeed for many women today, the Church is part of the problem..."[12]

The Churches and Reconciliation

Conflicts are often about who has power and whose voice is heard when decisions are made. Even the most cursory look at the pyramidal structure of the Roman Catholic Church shows that the system which cascades information easily downwards from the top to the bottom has had 2000 years of growth and development. There is no equivalent system for the upward flow of information. The laity have few structured avenues for "feedback" and contribution to decision-making. All decision-making rests in the hands of men since power within the church is attached like a limpet to priesthood and priesthood is attached like a limpet to maleness. Little wonder then with so few avenues through which to make their voices heard those who have something to say at the bottom have to shout loudly in order to be heard at all. Little wonder too that those inside the citadel are affronted at the stridency of those shrieking people outside! This is no way to honour the commandment to love each other. The institutional church's refusal to engage in serious and structured listening never mind debate is the response of an institution with a serious communication problem.

For many people looking at the conflict in Northern Ireland the churches are also part of the problem. In over identifying with their own flocks, in appearing only to bleed when their own are hurt, they have submitted to a disfigured gospel of exclusion rather than inclusion. They are not however the whole problem. The quirky mix of political ambitions, constitutional conflict, ethnicity and history have created a tangled web in which religion is only one of a number of key factors.

How did we Christians manage to get so comprehensively messed up? Answering that part is relatively easy. We learnt how to mess up comprehensively from St. Peter our very fallible first Pope. What is much more important to ask is how we can untangle the mess? What are each of us prepared to bring to the process of untangling and unlearning.

Shouting across the barricades rarely made anything clear. Shouting may make us feel strong and tough but we know it is bravado not bravery. Sometimes when we feel the ground beneath us shifting we cling ever tighter to it, fearful of where the uncontrollable surging forces will take us, afraid they may overwhelm us entirely. Our energies go into defensiveness. We become so worried, so busily consumed with worry that our sense of God's presence is put on hold. We will dwell in him but not yet. We will dwell in him when we get these enemies out of the way... Meanwhile there is the latest news bulletin to catch just in case the enemy have stolen a march on us. There are barricades to man rather than fences to mend.

I often think of the words of the most loved Pope of my lifetime Pope John XXIII (himself no great advocate of women's rights it must be said) but a man at least open to change and willing to create a climate of change.

"I am not here to guard a museum but rather to cultivate a garden."

Which do we want, to be curators or gardeners? Grass grows green and lush in silence, trees grow to majesty in silence. The flower opens in silence. God dwells in silence. It is where His embrace is most really felt. He dwells in noise too but while it does not distract Him from us we are certainly distracted from Him. We need to ask Him, to teach us how empty ourselves of all the noisy sediment and baggage we have gathered over a lifetime and which trips us up and blocks our path to Him, to teach us to accept that embrace which draws us right into His heart and makes our souls soar with the wonder of being loved so absolutely, so resolutely. May he also teach us accept that 'the other' is loved in exactly the same way. If God our Father and Mother offers such an embrace to 'the other' by what right do I, in God's Holy name dare to offer less?

FOOTNOTES CHAPTER 2.

1   Matt. 5: 43-46
2   "Sectarianism" A Discussion Document pub. Irish Inter-Church Meeting 1993
3   "World of Exclusion, Vision of Embrace" by Miroslav Wolf, paper delivered to Boundaries and Bonds Conference, Stranmillis College, Belfast, July 1997
4   "Whatever You Say Say Nothing" from "North" by Seamus Heaney pub. Faber and Faber 1975
5   Wolf, op. cit.
6   "John Main By Those Who Knew Him", ed. Paul Harris pub. Darton, Longman and Todd 1991
7   Wolf, op.cit.
8   "A Retreat With Thomas Merton – Becoming Who We Are" by Dr. A Padovano, pubs. Anthony Messenger Press 1995
9   "From The Canton Of Expectation" from "The Haw Lantern" by Seamus Heaney pub. Faber and Faber 1987
10 Address of Pope Paul VI in International Women's Year 1975
11 Letter of Pope John Paul II to women on the occasion of the U.N. Conference on Women
12 "Equality in Christ: Theological Reflections" Dr. D. Lane, in Women in the Church In Ireland – Proceedings of a Study Day 23.10.93 pub. Irish Commission for Justice and Peace

3

LEARNING THE DISCIPLINE OF LOVE

"I have a new commandment to give you, that you are to love one another"[1]

"This is my commandment that you should love one another as I have loved you. This is the greatest love a man can show, that he should lay down his life for his friends: and you, if you do all that I command you, are my friends. I do not speak of you any more as my servants; a servant is one who does not understand that his master is about, whereas I have made known to you all that my father has told me; and so I have called you my friends."[2]

Any pursuit of the idea of reconciliation leads to this commandment to love and the discipline it imposes us. Have we fully understood either the nature of that discipline or the nature of the friendship with God which we are privileged to be invited to?

In these two extracts from St. John's gospel Jesus is addressing the apostles at the Last Supper, the most important seminar of all time. He has just washed their feet. He has talked to them at length. His audience are raw uneducated people, the subject matter is complex and time is running out. A Ph.D. student in theology would have found his words hard going and every word matters. He is teaching them the discipline of love but even after 2000 years we are as baffled as the apostles. What will this thing called love look like, what will it feel like, what will it demand of us, how will we do it, how do we learn it?

Not ten minutes before the apostles had heard him say "You hail me as Master and Lord; and you are right, it is what I am." That made sense to them. He was their guru, their leader, they idolised him, would have done anything for him. Of course he was their Master. Like the good servants of all masters they sat waiting for orders, ready to jump to attention and do his bidding. Now they hear him say that he is their friend and so they are not his servants. You can almost hear the ones at the back of the class groan as they lose the plot.

What is happening at the Last Supper is quite extraordinary and seminal for the later Church. This is the first graduation class of Christian teachers. The Lord is saying – Look you started this process, as amateurs, as conscripts. I was the teacher, you the students. You did what you were told when you were told. At first you did not understand what I was about but now I expect you to have matured, to have deepened in understanding. Now you are going to be the teachers and you cannot teach with any credibility what you do not profoundly and comprehensively understand. To understand it you must do it, again and again and again until the subject you seek to master becomes a second nature to you. You are like soldiers coming to the end of a rigorous parachute training course. You are in the aeroplane for your first real drop and you are nervous as hell because the theory was all very fine but how can you be sure you will land in one piece. The commanding officer is the expert, the guru, the teacher. He knows that if you follow the rules you will be O.K. He also knows that left to your own devices you will hide under a seat and hope your turn will never come. He commands you to jump not just because he is the boss but because for him to be any good and for you to be any good you need to go through the experiential threshold of self-knowledge. You need to know that his teaching works for you and he needs to know that you know. You have to jump. Once you have landed, you now know for yourself. It works. One hundred jumps later you are the expert standing beside a nervous raw recruit. If you gently invite him to jump if he feels like it or when he feels like it chances are you will both still be in the plane when it lands.

Authority of Friendship

From our earliest days as children growing up in a Christian community we heard the word *commandment*. We learnt by rote the ten commandments, (though today's picky generation show every sign of having rounded them down to six); we recited the quaint phraseology, "Thou shall" and "Thou shalt not". As early as five or six years of age we told ourselves that we would not commit adultery or covet our neighbour's wives though we were clueless as to the meaning of the words. As words go they are powerful words, quite specific and unambiguous. They are words which we know are meant to bind us. There is a big difference between saying "I command you to do something" and saying "maybe you would consider doing such and such" or "I would like you to do such and such."

What is strange about Christ's commandment however is that he is commanding his friends. To command a friend to do something is in itself quite odd. Friends do not as a rule go around commanding each other to do things. A friend who commanded us would generally be an ex-friend very quickly. Commands usually emanate from someone in authority, someone who has power over another. Any Thesaurus given the word "command" will offer related words like "dominion", "domination", "supremacy", "lordship", "headship". None are likely to offer the word "friend". The relationship between the person commanded and the one commanding is presumed to be unequal and to carry with it a kind of distance, a formality which places both at arms length from one another. It is more like the relationship of master and servant. The servant is trained and disciplined to respond in a predictable way and does so. Indiscipline is intolerable in such relationships which depend on immediate and obedient response. The master has ways of making him conform if the response is not forthcoming. Master and servant relationships sometimes do grow into friendships but both parties know there is a line that separates them and circumstances may force one or both of them to toe that line.

Faced with that choice the friendship may have to be sacrificed.

Being in the Master's presence does not always mean being comfortable and at ease. It is not unknown after all, for the servant to fear the Master. Brian Keenan's captors had such a relationship with their God. The Old Testament is stuffed to the tips of its angels' wings with the most God-awful Gods imaginable. They thrash about smiting, avenging, dispatching bolts from the blue like pre-Christian Exocets and generally being very unfriendly. People hide from them. People tremble at the mere mention of their name and get out of their road sharpish. People submit to such a God because he is a great big bully who is mercifully on their side. This God encourages fear but he also encourages a peculiar kind of vehement faith, a zealotry which is always in imminent danger of spilling over into hatred. The Ulster poet John Hewitt describes such zealots as "creed-infected".

In his poem "Ulsterman" he speaks from the 'virtual' pulpit of "unfettered thought", a place outside of denomination for he despairs of denominationalism. Yet his words could be the words of Main or Merton or Cassian or de Caussade because they are a call to turn and face the hate, to name it, to out it, to deal with it and resolve it. He refuses to run away from it or from his ownership of the task of confronting it. The poem could be a metaphor for Main's meditation, for Wolf's Embrace or for the 18th century Jesuit De Caussade's "sacrament of the present moment". Prayer, stillness and contemplative silence are not escapes from reality though the temptation is to make them such. They are not bunkers to hide in. They are places in which we seek God's loving presence because we need that loving presence to make the world tolerable. We need the presence which contemplating discloses in order to fill us with spiritual energy, the courage to deal with all the circumstances that we are asked to deal with, whether sectarian hatred, whether death by religion, whether the cancer of a child or a spouse, whether the emotional freefall of self-doubt and depression, whatever form our personal Gethsemani may assume.

This is how Hewitt describes the Gethsemani of Northern Ireland;

> *"Though creed-crazed zealots and the ignorant crowd,*
> *long-nurtured, never checked in ways of hate,*
> *have made our streets a by-word of offense,*
> *this is my country, never disavowed.*
> *When it is fouled, shall I not remonstrate?*
> *My heritage is not their violence."*[3]

Here the faith of the zealots is immature, still-born, frozen in aspic. They have climbed no learning curve of spiritual growth. They are locked in the faith of the straitjacket, like Keenan's jailers who are themselves captives of their fanaticism. Hewitt by contrast, though he claims to have "forsworn the ailing church which claims dominion over the questing spirit..."[4] sounds more like a mystic, more Christ-like, more full of love than many willing servants of God. He has of course a poet's soul and stillness is to poets what water is to grass. Hewitt's mature understanding of the barrierlessness of God's world is very close to the model of understanding to which Christ is introducing his apostles in the seminar of the Last Supper. Barriers are inherent between master and servant and Jesus emphatically wants those barriers removed. This is why the issue of friendship is so crucial to the discipline of love, to the commandment to love.

The relationship between ordinary friends is altogether different from that of Master and servant. The Thesaurus asked to suggest words similar to or related to "friend" will offer words like "partner", "comrade", "companion", "chum", "confidant". Between friends there is closeness, intimacy, equality and informality. Friends usually like each other and may even trust each other enough to share great confidences. You might ask a great favour of a friend, one that requires selflessness on his or her part. But commanding a friend is something even a best friend would do with trepidation. Relationships in which one friend commands another to act in certain ways and in which the other meekly does as he or she is told, are today likely to be labelled unhealthy, co-dependent, immature and unbalanced. We might even describe the person issuing the command as a bully or a control freak. Who does he think he is to order me about?

So what is Christ up to then when he quite deliberately abandons the model of the master – servant relationship in which commands are normal and expected? What does he mean when he insists instead that his disciples have entered a bond of friendship with him but a bond in which he is by some quirk also Master. Can he truly be Master and friend? The answer is that, yes, he can for he is Master in the sense that he is the teacher, the expert, the repository of knowledge, that derives from experience. No-one knows his subject better than Christ. We his friends are invited to share that knowledge with him. The knowledge is quite simply that we are loved, that we can love each other and that love works. It does transform the world.

Why then does he command his friends to love one another? Because like the parachute instructor he knows that we are shivering with doubt, not just self-doubt but doubt about his credentials as a teacher, maybe about his very existence. He knows that if we try it we will like it, we will be amazed that it works but like Doubting Thomas we cannot be persuaded until we have done it ourselves. We are like the first time parachutist. We want to have a go. We have read up all the theory. It sounds great, exhilarating, but, Holy God, what are we doing 10,000 feet up in the air, looking out through the open door of an airplane. Are we mad or what? Its at precisely that point that we need someone to talk tough. We need someone to say – "You don't have to like it you just have to do it." We need the push, the command. We need to launch ourselves out into space and trust that the fellow barking the command knows what he is talking about. Everytime we go up in that plane for the next ten, twenty, thirty jumps we will feel sick with terror, unsure and miserable. But one day we will find ourselves sauntering to the open door, welcoming the rush of air, sure-footed even in freefall because we will have at last matured into people who spontaneously jump. The friend – master teaches us how to become people who spontaneously love and so who no longer need to be commanded.

It is a rare person who arrives at that state of perfect spiritual serenity. I suppose they are saints of sorts, not necessarily beatified and canonised saints but the kind of people in whose presence we intuit the nearness of God because they bring their best friend everywhere with them. God does not accompany them as a bodyguard or go in front of them like a Soviet tank clearing a path. He accompanies them like a soprano's pure voice accompanies a song, like a dewdrop sits on a rose. One such was Gordon Wilson. He was man so practiced in the discipline of love that when his beautiful daughter Marie died, hard and cruelly, at the slaughter that was the Enniskillen bombing, her hand in his as she slipped away, the words of love and of forgiveness sprang as naturally to his lips as a child's eyes are drawn to its mother. His words shamed us, caught us off guard. They sounded so different from what we expected and what we were used to. They brought stillness with them. They carried a sense of the transcendent into a place so ugly we could hardly bear to watch. But he had his detractors and unbelievably his bags of hate mail. How dare you forgive, they shouted? What kind of father are you who can forgive your daughter's killers? It was as if they had never heard the command to love and forgive anywhere before. It was as if they were being spoken for the first time in the history of humanity and Christ had never uttered the words, "Father forgive them for they know not what they do."As one church-going critic said to me on the subject of Gordon Wilson "Sure the poor man must have been in shock", as if to offer love and forgiveness is a sign of mental weakness instead of spiritual strength. If we are very very lucky we will meet one or maybe more than one such person in our lifetime, someone from whom we will catch love like a benign virus. The authenticity of their lives may teach us and challenge us to believe more fully, to make more effort at authenticity in our own lives. Or it may provoke us to contempt and cynicism.

Authority of the Home

There is a saying that what is learnt in childhood is engraved on stone. Parents are the first educators, probably the first to speak the name of God to the little child, the first to teach it how to pray and how to love. The danger is that in handing on "the faith" what in fact we hand on is our faith, perfect or imperfect, mature or immature. When we hand on the commandment to love, there is always the danger that we qualify it, thou shalt love those whom I command you to love and thous shalt hate those whom I command you to hate.

The crucible of tolerance is the home. The crib of hatred is the home. If mammy and daddy are passionately hostile to prods, fenians, Irish, Brits, Blacks, Jews, gays, snobs, cornerboys, travellers, northerners, southerners, feminists, sexists, you can be sure little Johnny will become passionate about them too. He loves his mum and dad. He wants to be like his mum and dad. They laugh and pat him on the head when he repeats their words, their phrases, their passions, their prejudices. The same mammy and daddy who love him and who teach him how to hate so subtly that they do not even notice themselves doing it, are also statistically at least in Northern Ireland, likely to be people of staunch faith. They will teach him how to pray. They will introduce him to a God who commands Christians to love – but not to love everybody. A God who is in agreement with their views on politics and prejudices and is in fact the source of both. If there is hypocrisy they do not see it. If there is contradiction they do not acknowledge it. The fracturing and distorting of truth becomes normal to the growing child. This God is a great supporter of mine. He is already just like me and so I have to make no effort to be like him!

Some time ago walking past the Presbyterian church in my home village my son, then aged five or six asked me; "Mammy do you know Catholics and Protestants? Which ones are we, I forget." Yet it seems it is an essential part of growing up, to remember. We are not permitted to forget. We put a lot of effort into teaching identity, to making sure we get the nuances just right, that we teach our children to crack the code of their own group. The "handgrips winks and nods", as Seamus Heaney describes them are handed on carefully like batons in a relay race which has no finish line.

Do we put as much effort into teaching prayer as we do into teaching the code that allows us to love conditionally and selectively? I asked my twelve year old daughter Sara Mai to describe prayer. "Its a bit like using a Help line, like Childline she said. You have a problem, you ring the Prayerline to God and ask him to sort it out. If he doesn't deliver in a reasonable time you ring him back and give out." The only thing missing in this view, is a Prayer Ombudsman to whom we can refer complaints about God's handling of our request. It's an even more sophisticated form of communication than e-mail or the world wide web. Telepathic troubleshooting!

That image of prayer is painfully familiar. This is prayer understood as a commando raid on God's headquarters rather than a leisurely visit to a friend's home. Gimme this, this and this, right now, this minute. Even the traditional devotional prayers, the Our Father and the Hail Mary which we love and use so often are couched in a wheedling mode familiar to the mother of any daughter or perhaps even more familiar to their daddies. First you butter God or daddy up. Hallowed be they name. Daddy I love you. Thy Kingdom come. You are the best daddy in the world. Give us this day our daily bread. "Daddy you should see the cool white patent Doc Marten boots in the shopping centre. They'd look great with the horrible confirmation dress that mammy bought me. Please..." This is followed by a fairly non-prayerful dialogue between mother and father later that night. "You bought her WHAT?"

Many years ago when Emma was small I was going over her night prayers with her. These generally took the form of asking Gods Blessing individually for everyone she knew. Please God, Bless Nanny and Granda and mammy and daddy. Suddenly she stopped. Her tone darkened. "No don't bother blessing daddy. He was mean to me today. He wouldn't buy me sweets so I don't want you to bless him"

Already and insidiously the seeds of a wheedling, cajoling, selfish prayer life were developing. If left unchecked, if no other form of prayer had been nurtured who or what would help the developing spirit to grow together with the growing body? In the Cloud of Unknowing the writer says "God forbid that I should separate what God has coupled, the body and the spirit."[4]

It is this prayer of petition, of always looking to get something, this essentially egotistical prayer which is the style of prayer we are most familiar with from childhood on. We may never move on from it or expand into deeper prayer. Laurence Freeman rightly criticises modern education for over-relying on "adequate regurgitation of facts and instilled opinions." He could have added that what passes for education in prayer is often not a lot better. This is not to meant to denigrate petitionary prayer but simply to address its narrowness as a basis for growing into a profound friendship with God. If we keep seeing him as an Argos catalogue God who delivers to order we make ourselves mere consumers of God's products rather than friends mutually engaged in a long spiritual journey.

I learnt a hard lesson on this subject several years ago, one December 8th. The Feast of the Immaculate Conception fell on a weekday and I was trying to prise my youngest daughter out of bed to go to Mass. A nun friend of mine had once described this innocent child as a congenital atheist! At the time I thought the judgment was a little premature as the child was barely four but her insistence that my nun friend tell her exactly where God was standing when he made the world had ended in a clear win for the junior team. I approached the bed with some uncertainty. I had never wanted to be the mother who said things like – "While you are under my roof you'll go to Mass and Confession and Devotions like a decent Christian!" But I had that ammunition in my belt just in case. First I told her it was a Holy Day. We were obliged to go. I didn't make the rules but the rules were the rules. She asked me did Protestants go to Church on Holy Days of Obligation. I replied, no. And God doesn't mind? she innocently enquired. I didn't feel authorised to speak on behalf of God. So I tried another tack altogether. Look I said on this day twenty years ago when I lived at home in Belfast with my mammy and daddy, bad men came to our house with machine guns and they tried to kill us. They didn't succeed thanks to Our Blessed Lady, so the least we could do today is thank her for the help she gave us all those years ago on the Feast of Her Immaculate Conception. Her eyebrows arched. She pulled the duvet over her head and announced – "Huh – sounds more like immaculate coincidence to me!"

Later I got to thinking about the encounter. I had done her, God and Our Lady an awful disservice. I had fallen into the trap of leading this child to believe that Our Lady had deliberately stopped the bullets because we were special. So when the bullets didn't stop, when there were dead bodies, what did that mean, what did that say about God? God sits up there playing real life Game Boy with a remote control device, zapping people? Is he telling his angels, we'll have those two Tutsis and that Catholic on the left but leave that one on the right. When my father did not die in the explosion designed to kill him but the mother of two young children did, was God choosing favourites, protecting some and ignoring others? What child would want to believe in such a volatile, untrustworthy, capricious God.

I revised not just the way I told the story of the sectarian attack on my family but I tried to deepen my own understanding. Yes, Our Lady was important to us that day. Not because she prevented several dozen bullets from hitting their intended targets but because she and her Son enveloped us in their loving presence, dwelt closely by us at a time when we felt frightened beyond belief and lonely beyond words. We had to deal with anger. They helped us do that. We had to deal with fear. They helped us to do that. We had to deal with trauma which ambushed us in different ways and at different times for many years to come. They helped us through all that. And later when our friends were murdered it was not because a loving God decided not to intervene on their behalf but because evil men just did a better and more efficient job than they did on us.

I realised I was unthinkingly introducing my children to the Lotto School of Prayer. I was treating God as the keeper of the Holy Lotto Balls who can bring my numbers up if I ask and if he chooses. Everytime something bad happened were my children going to think, "This is God doing this to me?" Or were they going to feel that God would be with them whatever befell them. How far is the wheedling, self-centred kind of prayer from the prayer that leads to a discovery of in-dwelling presence and to the spiritual broadening and deepening Christ called his disciples to when he made them friends rather than pathetic supplicants. The kind of prayer you need when you walk out into the air and trust in God's commandment to jump. John Main once said "We no longer benefit as we should from the wisdom and experienced counsel of the great masters of prayer." He is right in that. What we also fail to utilise is the gift of silence, even in our own homes, even in teaching our own children.

In our home the children are more likely to be shushed into silence so that we can hear the News than introduced to silence as a means of experiencing the presence of Christ. Two or three years ago Northern Ireland suffered a massive electricity black-out. It was a very dark winter's night. We found a candle and lit it. After some initial chatter about the situation we all gradually succumbed to the silence. It seemed to have a strange gravitational pull. The minutes seemed to be longer, thicker, wider, minutes of more dimensions than the thin, frenetic minutes we were accustomed to when the TV was blaring and the room glared with light. The spell grew until the moments took on a quality of sacredness. When the light suddenly snapped on and the TV jumped back to centre stage there was a palpable feeling of disappointment and loss. Those were the most fully lived moments for many a long day. They happened by accident not by design but we could change and could be taught to change accident into discipline.

The discipline of prayer, the discipline of love are like all disciplines. They demand a certain amount of order, of restraint and regulation. They do not become enriching parts of our lives by accident. People make them happen. There are those who turn their lives over entirely to detachment from the world of doing and busyness to the world of prayer and spirit. There are also those of us who have lives which are necessarily busy and noisy and full of tyrannical deadlines. Sure we can diary in periods of stillness, squeeze in space for meditation. But is that all prayer is to become, the half hour after step aerobics and before Coronation Street?

Doesn't the search for stillness call for a much greater involvement of the self? Jean Pierre de Caussade put it this way over two hundred and fifty years ago.

> "*God still speaks us today as he spoke to our forefathers in days gone by, before there were either spiritual directors or methods of direction. The spiritual life was then a matter of immediate communication with God. It had not been reduced to a fine art nor was lofty and detailed guidance to it provided with a wealth of rules, instructions and maxims. These may very well be necessary today. But it was not so in those early days, when people were more direct and unsophisticated. All they knew was that each moment brought its appointed task, faithfully to be accomplished. This was enough for the spiritually minded of those day. All their attention was focused on the present, minute by minute; like the hand of a clock that marks the distance along which it has to travel. Constantly prompted by divine impulse, they found themselves imperceptibly turned*

*towards the next task that God had ready for them at each
hour of the day."*[5]

The first time I read that I thought of my paternal grandmother.
She lived poorly and frugally in a tiny farm in the West of Ireland.
The richest aspect of her life was her faith and in particular her
prayer life. She walked several miles each day to morning mass,
winter and summer. By the time I got to know her she had turned
so consciously towards the task of going to morning mass that she
rose earlier and earlier each day until she established the custom of
arriving at the church an hour early. The priest left the key under
the stone for her. She would enter the still dark chapel, light a
candle, say the Stations and then sit in the candlelight until Mass
began. At first I thought her strange. Later I was grateful for her
strangeness and for the gift of her teaching though in fact she never
once explained to me what she was doing or why. But I knew even
then that in the stillness there was a source which gave her courage
and hope and meaning. She could not wait to meet her friend. She
wanted to spend as much time in his company as possible to learn
from him the feel of love and the way of living by his
commandment to love.

John Main says meditation is caught not taught. I agree and
disagree with that statement. The powerful witnesses to God's love,
whose lives intrigue us and whose ways we decide to imitate are
themselves great teachers. They need never say a word or explain
what they are doing. Their very strength lies in the way they have
managed to grow from being awkward amateurs practising how to
love, to become accomplished experts for whom loving has become
second nature. I like to think that my grandmother and other
women of her generation, who, as women, had been consigned to
silence, discovered that those who had imposed the silence on them
as a form of control had not understood the spiritual meaning of
silence. In the blindness of the oppressor they had thrown away a
pearl of great price. While some women passively accepted the
silence as a sign that they were of no value yet others turned it into

a place of deep-running bitterness. My grandmother colonised and nurtured the place of silence in her life. She explored it. She found there the presence of a loving God. And in silence she shared the secret of that gift with me. I took a long time to recognise the legacy she had given me. She was many years dead when her meditative prayer in the early morning chapel half-light, rang distant bells in my head. Like a gardener planting a seed she knows will only flower, if at all, after she is dead, she planted it in hope.

That is the discipline we are called to. To plant love in hope and to be fully prepared to see no apparent results in others in our own lifetime. Just as Christ, our friend and Master taught us by the example of his own life and death. God's timescale is not ours.

FOOTNOTES CHAPTER 3.

1 John 13: 34
2 John 15: 11-16
3 "Ulsterman" from "The Collected Poems of John Hewitt"
   ed. F. Ormsby pub. The Blackstaff Press 1991
4 "The Cloud of Unknowing" pub. Hodder and Stoughton 1985
5 "Sacrament Of The Present Moment" by Jean-Pierre de Caussade,
   pub. Fount Paperbacks 1996

4

PRACTISING LOVE IN CHAOS

"Most of the multitudes spread their garments along the way, while others strewed the way with branches cut down from the trees. And the multitudes that went before him and that followed after him cried aloud, Hosanna for the son of David, blessed is he who comes in the name of the Lord, Hosanna in heaven above. When he reached Jerusalem, the whole city was in a stir."[1]

"Pilate said to them What am I to do then, with Jesus who is called Christ? They said Let him be crucified."[2]

They say a week is a long time in politics. The week between Palm Sunday and Good Friday was one of the longest in Christendom. On Palm Sunday the disciples could have been forgiven for thinking that the love Christ talked about was what we would call the feel-good factor. Jerusalem was chaotic, pure pandemonium. But there is chaos and chaos. This was the chaos of a big party. It was carnival time. The mood was festive and fun. Jesus, their leader and hero, entered Jerusalem to a tumultuous welcome. He was mobbed like a modern popstar. People threw their garments on the street to welcome him. They carried branches of palm like flags of welcome. "Hosanna" they shouted. "Blessed is he who comes in the name of the Lord."

It is not hard to imagine what the disciples were thinking. The place was buzzing with Jesus' name. There were smiles on the faces of the multitudes. The support of the crowd was tangible and touching. "Yes" they were thinking to themselves. "We have achieved our goal! What could possibly go wrong after a day like this? We have arrived at our destination! From now on every day will be like this."

But what was Christ thinking amidst all this adulation? In his magnificent poem "Resurrection" W.R.Rodgers suggests a sharper, uglier view of the occasion was forming in Christ's head.

> "... and when at last he appeared
> – the hero – such a hail of huzzas and hosannahs as sprang up.
> Why the very housetops rose to the occasion and broke
> Their hush and hung out all their hearts' hoorays.
> This was glory. Yet he knew the swings of men and now it
> was the old story.
> Those who magnified now would mock him tomorrow,
> Those who deified, defy.
> Already he saw
> The shadow of doubt, that pickpocket of conviction
> Move through the crowds. And far away behind
> Their fume and furore of glory he heard the door
> Of doom slam: Meanwhile all was gay
> And like a King he came triumphant on his way."[3]

No self-respecting bookie would have given this tiny Christian sect the remotest chance of surviving past Easter Sunday. The leader was dead. His followers were in hiding. The establishment was against them, the crowd hated them. Everything about them smacked of abject failure. Peter the rock on whom the church was to be founded was the most cringe-making and undignified of them all, a coward and a liar.

Six days later many in that same crowd bayed for his blood and delighted in his agony. The high tide of hope and happiness which had flushed all doubt from the minds of the disciples ebbed as dramatically as it surged, sucking them out into a tormented sea of despair and panic. The frail feel-good hope of Palm Sunday had proved to be transient and treacherous. It had been so easy to hope when people were clapping you on the back, embracing you with palms and Hosannahs. But now that the same crowd oozed and spewed hatred for the self-same thing they had applauded, where was hope? The effect on the apostles was tragic. The big important men of Palm Sunday were now shrunken, small and insignificant. Though they did not fully know it, they were hovering on the brink of the world's most extraordinary revelation. They were about to discover that if there was hope at all then it was a shockingly different kind of hope from that experienced on Palm Sunday. Their "cloud of unknowing" was about to be transfigured by tongues of fire. After Pentecost they knew that they were not only the work of God's hands but they were now the hands of his work. Shaky hands, feeble shoulders, but hands without which the work could not be done. The intoxicating giddiness of Palm Sunday was a sham and a tacky illusion. For one daft silly moment they had believed the Gospel could be lived without any more effort than that required to wave to a happy crowd. Now they knew the gospel would have to be lived in the hard places. The ugly chaos of the world around them was their workplace. Failure was their bed. The Palm Sunday spree was over.

The poet Patrick Kavanagh describes what can happen to a person whose life is sunk in defeat and in failure.

From Failure Up

"Can a man grow from the dead clod of failure
Some consoling flower
Something humble as a dandelion or a daisy,
Something to wear as a buttonhole in Heaven?
Under the flat, flat grief of defeat maybe
Hope is a seed
Maybe this's what he was born for, this hour
Of hopelessness.
maybe it is here he must search

In this hell of unfaith
Where noone has a purpose
Where the web of meaning is broken on threads
And one man looks at another in fear."[4]

Belfast Easters

There have been "Palm Sunday Days" in every conflict. We have had them in Belfast; days when we believed the seed of hope had finally blossomed and that all was suddenly about to be well. Peace People marched, doves of peace were released, we held hands and sang hymns which offended neither side. One such day happened in November 1995 when we clamoured our welcome to President Clinton. Even the sourest and most distrustful of faces grew wide with smiles as the party mood infected the country gripping us with a wild mad joy. He turned on the Christmas lights and had our heads full of jingling bells. People prattled on and on about new hope and new eras, of problems solved, of people reconciled.

I thought of Rodgers Resurrection and wondered what the truth really was. The mood was not long evaporating. A Catholic friend said sourly. "The Brits are hopping mad he's here at all. He's on our side no doubt about that but of course he has to play to both audiences." A Protestant teacher friend asked his class of six year olds if they had enjoyed the Clinton visit. One cherub answered. "My ma says he's an oul Fenian[5] lover!" And somewhere close by, quiet groups of men were saying "Prime the bombs, get the guns greased. The Clinton party is over."

One voice of hope stood out for me. It came in a curious place and from a curious source. Someone broke the mood of welcome by shouting "No Surrender" at the President. The episode got a lot of coverage on radio and TV. Not reported, at all, was the voice that emerged from the silence, a voice from a member of the same community " Why don't you go away back to Jurassic Park where you belong?" Not quite the full gospel but a good start!

And so we faced into another Christmas that year. The newborn infant was feted with expensive gifts as the peace process disintegrated before our tightshut eyes. By Easter 1996 he was crucified again. The remorseless hate seemed as cyclical as ever.

The poet Yevtushenko once said "Who never knew the price of happiness will not be happy." It has been said that too many of us in Northern Ireland chose to make ourselves as selfishly comfortable and cocooned as possible. We preferred to accept the chaos around us rather than pay the personal price of happiness. In his poem "The Coasters" the ethnic "Protestant" poet John Hewitt turned a contemptuous tongue on his own people accusing them of coasting along, contenting themselves with the superficial and the egoistical until it was too late to turn back from the precipice.

> *"You coasted along.*
> *And all the time, though you never noticed,*
> *the old lies festered;*
> *the ignorant became more thoroughly infected;*
> ....
> *the cloud of infection hangs over the city,*
> *a quick change of wind and it*
> *might spill over the leafy suburbs.*
> *You coasted too long."*[6]

He was prophetic. They did indeed coast too long, ignoring the looming crisis and the infection did eventually spill over. They passed by on the other side, indifferent. But on the other side (my side) dangerous myths and practices coasted along too. The infection of resentful martyrdom and the myth of the nobility of the blood sacrifice grew louder. It made our gethsemani a battlefield. We acted as if the Lord had said to his apostles when one of them cut off the ear of the high priest's servant "Right lads get stuck in. Fight to the death to protect your God and to vindicate him. Our cause is righteous, theirs profane. Our killing is good killing, theirs is bad." In fact he had responded by saying;

> *"Put thy sword back into its place. All who take up the*
> *sword shall perish by the sword."*[7]

We had all learnt those words. At least we had all heard them. But other words competed with them, contradicted them and for a while coerced them into whispers. To paraphrase Kenneth Kaunda, "We ransacked the memory for occasions of bitterness and resentment". We kept candles burning under them so that they would always be on simmer ready to be turned up to full heat when necessary. We also neutralised the effect of our side's actions. Contrary to the advice of the Cloud of Unknowing we did indeed separate body and soul. With specially constructed phrases we refused to see the sectarianism in killing policemen. They were we contended, a partisan militia, part of the forces of the Crown, soldiers in a war and therefore legitimate targets. We told ourselves that our side's bombs were much less profane and barbarous than the slitting of throats, the kickings to death favoured by the sectarian thugs of militant loyalism. Those who used bombs and bullets had a genuine clinical distance about them which made them superior to the bully boys whose feet trashed Catholic bodies. Our intentions were purer because, after all, God was on our side. Instead of practicing love in chaos we added to the chaos by practising dissembling and the language of denial. "Not me Lord" we said. "If you want to find the source of the problem look over there at those 'others', what a thoroughly bad lot they are." We learnt to live in a bilingual and bifurcated world where we could quote the gospel with one tongue and deny it with the other. We condemned the violence out of one side of our mouths and condoned it with the other. We lived in a world of shock not a world of wonder. Christ became shockingly paraphrased.

That is not to say we did nothing. We prayed, catholics and protestants, even praying together occasionally. A virtual industry of cross community initiatives grew up with some at real cost to the individuals concerned. A simple Christmas hand-shake in Limavady between a Protestant pastor and a Catholic priest registered ten on the ecclesiastical Richter Scale; the pastor was forced to leave defeated but defiant. Hundreds of small, medium and large cross-community initiatives have been started, many with great ambitions; some foundered, some still struggle and some have achieved real success. The children's school curriculum educates them for mutual understanding. Coachloads of children from different communities have been taken on holidays together to discover their common humanity, to befriend each other. We have chased reconciliation rainbows up hill and down dale, embracing all sorts of gambles and notions but Alan Boesak's words from South Africa ring very true.

> "Reconciliation is not holding hands and singing "Black and white together'. Reconciliation is not blacks and whites going to summer camp together.... and then returning to our separate and separated lifestyles. Reconciliation is not merely feeling good, but doing what is right."[8]

What kind of doing does he mean? Aren't the ecumenical bus runs also "doing". Isn't it 'doing' when bishops set up forums for dialogue with women? The key to understanding what Alan Boesak means lies in a phrase Mother Teresa uses in a different context when she says that what is demanded of us as Christians is that we "give until it hurts." This has to be right, doesn't it, for the Cross of Christ is the ultimate form of giving until it hurts, self-giving to the point of total self- abandonment to the other, especially if they are on the other side

There are forms of well-meaning social reconciliation which make us look and sound busy and full of the doing of good things. But they rarely stretch us to the full distance demanded by the gospel. That is not to denigrate their importance. They are important building blocks, crucial starting points on the way to a more demanding "giving and doing" but they are not substitutes for it. Concepts such a parity of esteem, fair employment, equality of treatment, equality of opportunity have to be real in their consequences not just pretty in their rhetoric. These are concepts which mature Christians should readily recognise as no less than what the gospel demands. But in a conflict society or institution where power is skewed in favour of one group or one gender, Christians often go from cradle to grave in a state of morbid anxiety. They are terrified that every gain made by the 'other' is made at their expense. Why should they settle for equality when inequality gives the bigger share? And when God himself backs that inequality, well it must be alright mustn't it?

The hard evidence is that once people start to accept that genuine reconciliation can only be built on an honest acknowledgment firstly that inequality exists and secondly that its effects must be addressed, two things happen. First the forces of resistance muster. They have been programmed to squeal like stuck pigs when their dysfunctional boat is rocked. Secondly, intelligent, thinking people in the rocking boat start to question the wisdom of squealing so loudly. They begin to listen to the 'other' and to agree that he or she does after all have a point. A quiet dialogue takes place against the background of the din of dissent. Over a period of time the squealers begin to notice that they are losing volume. Not as many people are squealing any more. Some of them have merely gone silent, given up in the face of the inevitable. Others have been persuaded that change that is coming and it is something they could and should embrace.

I believe we are close to that stage both in the politics of Northern Ireland and in the politics of the Church. It is perhaps the most dangerous stage of all. Groups are no longer the comfortable places they once were. Identities once fixed are now more fluid. Friends and family who used to think and speak with one mind and voice are now more differentiated, more at odds with one another. The challenge to the group is no longer just from outside. It is now from within too. It is dangerous because its very momentum can frighten us into slinking back into the old solidarity, the old ways. Being habitually distrustful of 'the other' our antennae are still tuned to any evidence of his perfidy. Give us an excuse and we will start to squeal again.

It is sadly ironic that as we have slowly come to believe in real equality, whether political, social, economic, spiritual or gender, the churches have rarely been seen as major advocates of change. I would even say that submission to the discipline of equality legislation in the field of employment has done more to promote benign culture change than submission to the discipline of the Gospel.

Two decades ago workplaces all over Northern Ireland became constrained by a code of Fair employment which was designed to redress the scandal of imbalance under which job chances for catholics were considerably lower than those for protestants. Similar legislation protects people from discrimination in jobs on account of their gender, race or disability. Employers and employees have had to look hard at employment practices and face difficult questions about equality of access to jobs and the neutrality of the working environment. People had to be retrained. Their work practices were opened up to public gaze, scrutinised by the courts and measured against the standards set by the legislation. They learnt about their hidden baggage, how to recognise it and how to deal with it.

The law does not require us to like what we do. We just have to do it. After a while though, doing it becomes the norm. Like it or not we begin to shape our thinking to match our doing. Soon we "do" because we think differently. In the field of employment reform in Northern Ireland there have been forces of resistance but undoubtedly there has also been a seismic shift. Things have not stayed still. Views once compacted like hard-core sediment have begun to soften. More people are becoming uncomfortable with their own old ways of thinking.

On the political front there is evidence of this changing mood which it is important to acknowledge, nurture and protect from the infection of cynicism. These small but perceptible shifts are precious, but precarious stepping stones to the full embrace we all long for. The old monoliths are fragmenting, each new grouping a sign of the level of discomfort with old myths and perspectives. The loyalist Ulster Democratic Party and the Progressive Unionist Party now engage in robust political discourse which is refreshingly free of the sectarian overtones and sneering verbal violence of the past. They now routinely challenge the verbal terrorism which can fuel conflict as effectively as physical violence. Maybe soon the language of the golf club, the coffee morning and the dinner table will follow suit. Sinn Fein set out their negotiation stall but indicate that they are prepared to work towards a consensus which will be less than their deepest ambition for a united Ireland. The paramilitary cease-fires show too how perspectives can turn around. Cynics snarl "tactical". Tactical or not they change the landscape. They give a space in which raw wounds get time to heal instead of becoming re-infected. It is important that when we hear good news and see it happen that we counter the tendency to dismiss and zap it with disdain. Reverencing every sign of hope has to be part of practising the gospel of love in the chaos. Love also means looking out for the tiny green shoots of hope, seeing in them the presence of the God we believe in and giving them help to grow to fruition.

If 1997 was a summer of discontent it was also a summer of some stunning examples of good 'doing' practice. Christians of all denominations stood hand in hand at Harryville when Catholics ran a gauntlet of abuse on their way to Saturday evening mass. People challenged 'their own' side in public. Their generosity opened up some intriguing space. The parish priest set aside the rights of his people to their Saturday Mass in order to reduce the temperature in a potentially hot summer. Not everyone on his side was pleased but this kind loving in chaos hurts. It can cut to the bone. Interestingly however, no sooner had one gesture of reconciliation happened than we heard calls for a reciprocal act of generosity. There was an intuitive awareness of a natural law which demands that generosity be rewarded with generosity.

Christians might see this for what it is the, multiplying power of love. Each act of love, of giving, almost spontaneously demands reciprocation. Each side offers help when their respective schools and churches and halls are burnt. Some communities quietly and unobtrusively maybe even miraculously work through to a consensus on marches in their area. The Church of Ireland debates its relationship with the Orange Order. The Orange Order opens itself up to difficult internal debate where colleague is pitted against colleague. It looks afresh at its relationship with the political parties. An awful darkness precedes the march at Drumcree but there is no sustained triumphalism when Orange feet go down that road. The Orange Order chooses not to march on the Ormeau Road or in other places of contention that same week. The Ulster Unionist Party starts a process of community consultation and invites the Catholic Church into that process. The unthinkable starts to happen.

Patterns of behaviour once set in concrete, alter just enough to create a tiny precedent on which to build. Those who are working tirelessly to bring about an IRA cease-fire are successful. We hold our breaths. Cynics make their verbal commando raids trying to drain the good out of these small 'doings'. And there is plenty to break our hearts and leave us wallowing in disappointment. Sectarian deaths continue, punishment beatings continue, the language of conflict continues. But each little nudge forward is a giant step up the learning curve. In the midst of chaos we begin, just begin, to see the leavening power of even the littlest bit of love. There is a long road to travel yet but now hope has begun to sprout green shoots. There are tantalisingly uncertain talks about talks, inclusive or exclusive. Our futures ride on carefully finessed words. The jumbled politics of the North, like a tangled ball of wool is being carefully untangled by a herd of spitting cats. We veer unsteadily towards hope but are always liable to race backwards to despair. Can we ever move from winners and losers to winners and winners?

God Has No Favourites

For this progress in reconciliation to happen, no-one has actually to name love as his motive. It is possible to do things which have good consequences while our hearts badly want to do the opposite. That tension is exactly the tension Christ implants. He knew the apostles were cowards at heart. He knew they needed to be cajoled, pushed, commanded. He knew that over time they would lose their fear and gain understanding but not until they had moved from their immature, inhibited, amateur mentality. Every tentative move they made in his direction had to be prised out of them, but when it came he praised it and so strengthened their confidence in themselves and in him. More importantly, while he often gently chided them when they let him down, he did not dump such a mountain of disdain and condemnation on them that he ruptured relationships with them. Always he tempered his upset and disappointment with his unconditional love, his ready forgiveness.

Among the main players on the stage of conflict politics in Northern Ireland, as in other conflicts around the globe, there are some people of profound peace but many more of an uncertain and insecure personal peace. The peace making process has to be pursued with the tools and personalities at hand. In using these imperfect resources we have to be prepared for set-backs and delays. It is important to understand that the Christian gospel is on the line in such processes in a very real way. There are those who will say that the gospel is also on the line in the debate about the exclusion of women in the Catholic Church. Some people argue that what is at stake is not the gospel but institutional churches. However institutional churches purport to embody the gospel and to be shop-windows for Christ. In Northern Ireland two ordained ministers and a lay preacher are among the seventeen public representatives elected to Parliament. The rest all claim allegiance to the gospel of Christ. They are all members of one Christian denomination or another. So are those who vote for them. We are a church-going people. Four thousand marches are held annually, many of them marches to church. Church services have been picketed and worshippers spat on, vilified and roughed up on their way to and from church. There is a cacophony of God talk but a lot of it has broken relationships down instead of building them up. If the gospel is a common language, a common homeland, a place where friend sits down with friend, a place where God's love dwells, the cynics could rightly say the signs of it have been well hidden.

The fundamental and intractable constitutional and political conflict still remains. This is after all a dispute about ownership of the land of the North of Ireland, a not unfamiliar dispute in the post-colonial, post imperial era. It is a serious dispute. There are two opposite points of view. There are two ambitions which on the face of it will be impossible to reconcile unless one or both concede some ground. But reconciling those political ambitions is not in itself the challenge facing the Christian churches. The challenge for the Churches is to take the sectarian hatred out of the political discourse, to leave the politics and remove the poison. The fact is God loves all sides equally. The fact is he is neither Unionist nor Nationalist, Fianna Fail nor Fianna Gael, Labour nor Tory. The fact too is that not enough people acknowledge these facts in the deepest part of their being. Too any people hold desperately to the conviction that God is a Catholic and an Irish nationalist, that he is a Unionist and a British Protestant, that he is Jewish and Israeli, Muslim and Palestinian. The use of His name as a form of scaffolding for prejudice has to end.

Who could blame those who like Hewitt feel they have to turn their backs on all churches and denominations in order to feel spiritually sane. It is tempting to say "A plague on all their houses" and to see them as beyond redemption. Yet there are those of us who love our churches with a pity and a compassion which does not allow us the freedom to turn away. They are our hearth and home. We want them to be places of open doors not locked vaults. We stay to do that work because as Newman said

"God has created me to do him some definite service. He has
committed one work to me which he has not committed to
another. I have my mission. I have a part in a great work. I
am a link in a chain, a bond of connections between persons.
He has not created me for naught. I shall do his work."[9]

By staying and working within our own denomination we do not
hold ourselves superior to any other. Many of us draw strength and
inspiration from our sister Christian churches and from the other
great world religions. The interface between the religions of the East
and West of which meditation is part is one of the most hopeful and
exciting dynamics in twentieth century spiritual growth.

Several weeks ago the newspapers carried an exciting story of a
major breakthrough in the field of genetics research. After many
fruitless and frustrating years scientists had succeeded in identifying
the gene which caused a particular form of severe mental disability.
The doctor who led the research team was asked to explain how he
and his colleagues had made the breakthrough. His answer was
instructive. For years he and other researchers in the area had
competed jealously and aggressively with each other to find the
flawed gene but they got nowhere. Finally they decided to stop
competing and to share all the knowledge they had between them.
Out of that sharing came the answer they had been looking for.

Though the researchers did not know it they were engaged in a
process of embrace. Each competing research team had created
space within itself to receive the other. By opening up that space,
ideas and insights previously blind to each other suddenly
recognised each other. Pieces which did not fit when they were kept
in separate spheres suddenly formed a meaningful pattern when put
together. This was truly a case of the whole picture being infinitely
greater than the sum of all the parts.

In a real sense they had managed to reconcile, to bring together
things which belonged together naturally but which might never
have found each other unless someone had decided to do the
unthinkable - to make friends of the "enemy". They were, after all,

looking for the same thing! Their uncoordinated, unintegrated bits of knowledge simply needed to be joined up. They only made sense when they were joined up. The years of labour only took on full meaning when the labourers were reconciled to each other.

The story could be a metaphor for the God-given complementarity of all humanity and for the need to free up the energy and wisdom of that complementarity by taking the risk of true embrace. It could be a metaphor for the conflict between men and women within the church. For as long as they are separate and unequal (or even separate and equal) we will have a lopsided, limping church, chugging along on one cylinder instead of firing on two. It could be a metaphor for peace processes in all ethnic or religious conflicts across the globe including that in Northern Ireland. No one side ever has a monopoly on truth or answers. Insisting on giving space to only one side's view is what got us into this mess in the first place. The future has to lie with a shared vision that comes out of a respectful pooling of views and pain and ambitions.

Christ calls us to practice his love in chaos because there is no other place. We do not get the time and place of our choosing. "You did not choose me. I chose you."

If we are going to be Christians it is here and it is now. This is our moment of sacrament. If it seems the job is too big and too complicated there are other encouraging words to remember,

> "In the world you will only find tribulation; but take courage, I have overcome the world."[10]

The last part is the bit we usually forget; the world has already been overcome by love.

My husband and I waited a long time for our first-born. When she eventually arrived I loved her with a passion so intense that an hour or a day without her was an hour or day wasted. I told her I loved her a hundred times a day. I still do. When she was about three or four she and I went shopping one day. She wriggled free of my hand to go and look at something that had caught her attention. She drifted seven or eight yards away from me. There were people and rails of clothing in between and lots of noise and bustle. I never took my eyes off her not even for a second but she lost sight of me. Suddenly she realised she could not see me. In an instant she had whipped herself into such a frenzy that she spun around like a cartwheel shrieking and screaming. The word "mammy" wailed across the store. By the time I got to her she was beyond consolation. If she had stayed calm, if she had just stopped panicking for a couple of seconds she would have seen me standing there close by and watching. She would have realised she was safe. But she was thrashing about too blindly to really see. Mammy had gone out of her world and everything around her was one big strange frightening mess. I picked her up, cuddled her and took her to the car. All the way home she sobbed and sobbed. "Why did you leave me mammy?" My heart was broken as I tried to convince her that I had not left her, that I had watched her every single moment, but still the little voice reproached me, "But where were you? Why did you go away?" "But Emma it was you who left me" I said. It did not matter. That is not how it felt to her.

So often that is how we are with God. We panic, spin around and around in desperation looking for him but our vision never focuses, it moves wildly and madly settling nowhere, unable to see him, unaware that it is we who have slipped away from him.

Dear Lord we might pray, you placed us in our own particular chaos for your own particular purpose. We are often afraid and unsure of ourselves, unclear about how much we can achieve and where we ought to start to practice what you taught. We are not the first to feel like this. We repeat the words of the philosopher Boethius written from prison almost 1500 years ago just before his distinguished career ended in ignominious execution.

> "O Thou who bindest bonds of things
> Look down on all earth's wretchedness;
> Of this great work is man so mean
> A part, by Fortune to be tossed?[11]

Lord hold the rushing waves in check
And with the bond Thou rul'st the stars,
Make stable all the lands of earth"[10]

FOOTNOTES CHAPTER 4.

1   Matt. 21: 8-10
2   Matt. 22: 23-24
3   "Resurrection" from "Poems" by W.R. Rodgers pub. Gallery Books 1993
4   "From Failure Up" from "The Complete Poems" by Patrick Kavanagh pub. The Goldsmith Press
5   The term "Fenian" is an abusive word for Catholics
6   "The Coasters" from "The Collected Poems of John Hewitt" ed. F. Ormsby pub. The Blackstaff Press 1992
7   Matt. 26: 52
8   "The Law of God" in "The Finger of God", by Alan Boesak, New York 1982
9   quoted in "In Pursuit of Happiness" by Richard Harries
10   John 1: 6: 33
11   "The Consolation of Philosophy" by Boethius, Penguin Classics

5

BUILDING A RECONCILED SELF

In his Letter to the Romans Paul tells the early Christians

"Adapt yourselves no longer to the pattern of this present world but let your minds be remade and your whole nature thus transformed."[1]

In Belfast we have things called 'peace lines'. We use words in quirky ways! A stranger hearing of a peace line might imagine a chain of people hand in hand singing songs of peace or a line beyond which there is a sanctuary of peace. These 'peace lines' are in fact robust security walls designed to keep people from getting at each other. They are the dangerous physical interface where faction lives beside faction not in the acknowledgment of each others common humanity which is supposed to result from living together but in the raw hatred that comes from forced cohabitation with people whom you despise or fear. Like a marriage gone badly wrong, where two sour spouses draw a line down the middle of the house to mark their respective territory, the fact that they live under the same roof is not evidence necessarily that they live in love. That is the nice definition. P.J. O'Rourke's is memorably more graphic.

"The Peace Wall is a kind of sociological toddler gate erected by the British to keep the ragamuffin Protestant homicidal maniacs of the Shankill Road away from the tatterdemalion Catholic murderers in Falls Road two blocks over."[2]

Walls of brick, barbed wire and steel separate Catholic ghetto from Protestant ghetto, Catholic neighbour from Protestant neighbour. They do not promote peace, they merely make violence a bit more difficult. They are incapable of changing hearts though their existence is evidence of hardened hearts. They can reroute violence but they cannot ultimately prevent hatred from seeping through the cracks.

Some Christians have deliberately chosen to locate themselves on the peace line to make it the place where they will do God's work. A number of small ecumenical communities have grown up in that no-man's land right on the boundary. They have quietly and unobtrusively colonised parts of the buffer zone. Their work looks like a drop in a very leaky bucket but better a drop than a complete drought.

One member of such a community describes their role this way

> "We are a Christian cry of protest against the brokenness that is symbolised by the physical barrier which tries to separate us; we are a sign of an alternative reconciled way of living together. Sometimes in the past we have hoped for an easy reconciliation without having to face up to the hard problems of political and social justice. My own conviction is that the barriers will not come down until there are political and legal structures that protect the essential human rights and traditions of both communities. But if these questions are to be courageously and honestly faced, there will have to be at the same time a process of human and religious reconciliation. Only that will allow us to lay aside animosity and anger, bitterness and bad blood; recognise how our own actions have contributed to the present situation and therefore our need to seek forgiveness. As a Christian I believe that it is only the reconciling power and Spirit of Christ that will free us to take the necessary risks. He is our peace, and communities like our own are signs of that power already breaking down the walls that would divide us."[3]

The work of groups like these are clear-cut examples of how Christians can consciously choose not to "adapt themselves to the pattern of the present world." The so-called peace barriers are designed to facilitate a pattern of separateness. They are a sorry acceptance that easy interface between the two communities in these areas is too fraught with real physical danger. The walls say, stick to your own side. But the ecumenical communities have shown that in Redmond Fitzmaurice's words 'the walls are permeable.' Hope does thrive on the hard work done between rocks and hard places. No-one claims these and thousands of other small initiatives are going to transform Northern Ireland. At most they are tiny pieces in the complex jigsaw puzzle which will eventually put together a country at peace with itself.

Many of those pieces have yet to be crafted. Some of the big pieces will be crafted by politicians and political parties but even those pieces will take their shape from the smaller pieces around them. There are a million and a half people in Northern Ireland and there are a million and a half such pieces. Who will decide the shape of those? Will I decide my own shape or will I let someone else shape it for me? Will history twist and tangle it so that it sits awkwardly and prevents completion of the whole picture or will I take control of the present moment, cut the umbilical cord to a past I cannot change and shape a piece which will fit easily into a consensual future?

Ultimately these choices are mine. It is worth asking where God will be when I make those choices. Whose words will he speak when I ask his help? Will I listen in humble silence while he speaks his own or will I hear him regurgitate mine? When I ask God to give us Peace will he reply to me as he did to the man who prayed that he would win the Lotto. "First help yourself-by a ticket" Is the answer to praying for peace likely to be- Tell me what practical thing you did for peace today?" There is a lovely image from a prayer of Dom Helder Camara which gives a clue to the potential that exists for change.

> "All absolutely all
> by your grace
> speaks to me of you.

When I write I ask in your name to be
The blank sheet of paper
Where you can write what you please."[4]

This is a powerful image that merits deeper reflection. In it the Christian empties himself so utterly to God and submits himself so openly to God's will that he becomes free of everything attaching him to the world. He simply becomes an open channel down which God's love flows. Nothing clogs up the channel because there is nothing in the world of such importance that it can be allowed to get in the way of the free-flow of God's grace. That kind of sensitivity to the will of God is easier to associate with the lives of those who have consciously renounced the world than with the busy lives of those of us who are buying designer label runners one minute and racing to Mass the next. How can we realistically detach ourselves from the pattern of this present world so that our minds can be remade and our natures transformed?

If Brian Keenan had sat in his cell for four years consumed with anger and thoughts of retribution who would have blamed him. He could have waited and prayed for his God to annihilate this Allah of Islamic Hezbollah. His story might made a great epic movie but there would have been no edifying inner journey. Ultimately what reconciles him to his situation is not a change in outward circumstances for they only get worse but his exploration of his inner self. It is a painful emptying of the self, a surrendering of the sort Camara describes and a surprise finding that the journey is not taken alone but in the presence of a love force, whom we would call God. Keenan did not create it he merely found it waiting where it had always been.

We Start From Here

Where do we each start this inward journey which centres us on love and ties up the frayed ends and fragments of our lives into a reconciled being? The simple answer is that we start from where we are. We are not looking for penetrating insights into mystery. We are not called to make great intellectual cartwheels. The gas chambers, the killing fields, the peace lines, the ups and downs of ordinary and extraordinary lives throughout humanity have been written about in graphic personal testimonies, analysed by historians, debated and discussed by students, measured by statisticians and explained by social scientists. There have been more fact-finding missions to Northern Ireland than there are facts, to paraphrase P.J.O'Rourke. They have produced an avalanche of questions, a modicum of wisdom and an amazing amnesia. They have generated innumerable solutions, proposed solutions and explanations. One unavoidable truth is that individuals have had to live through these days and nights. They have had to make their own sense of them and their own sense of God's place in them, first and foremost.

God calls us to take responsibility for our own lives, to stop driving everyone else's car vicariously and to bring about change in the little bit of reality we have responsibility for. We have some bad examples in this regard. The first bible story most of us learn is the squalid story of Adam and Eve. It is the first and very telling example of a husband blaming his wife for everything that goes wrong and of a wife covering up for her husband's inadequacy by blaming a third party. While the story is not exactly uplifting, the fact that it is apocryphal rather than real is no comfort for most of us know from everyday life that even if it did not happen this way it could easily have done so. The weasly Adam and blustering Eve are fairly familiar everyday characters. "Poor me." we lament "Life would be great if everybody lived the way I would like them to live, but because they don't there is no point in me even trying."

I have often wondered to what extent the problem of owning responsibility for conflict is genetically programmed. I learnt something about it through an incident in my twin's development. Aged two, they shared a bedroom. There was a bit of a communication problem in that I had an expectation that they would actually sleep in that room and they were determined that sleep was the last thing they would do. At bedtime they suddenly came to life and no matter how many times the light was turned off by some miracle it always turned itself on again. Eventually a law was decreed. Anyone found turning on the light after lights out would be subject to unspecified penalties. I waited outside their room. The conversation went like this.

> Sara to Justin. "Justin turn on the light."
>
> Justin, saint and self-preservationist," No, mammy will be cross"
>
> "Turn it on or I won't be your friend".
>
> "No mammy will be very cross."
>
> "Justin turn it on or I am going to thump you now!"
>
> Light goes on.
>
> Enter mother. "Who turned on the light"
>
> Sara "He did".

Sometime between childhood and adulthood we have to move out of "duck the blame" and "blame others" mode. We have to enter the"I am responsible for my bit mode".

Jean Pierre de Caussade says

> "All creatures live by the hand of God. The senses can only grasp the work of man, but faith sees the work of divine action in everything. It sees that Jesus Christ lives in all things, extending his influence over the centuries so that the briefest moment and the tiniest atom contain a portion of that hidden life and its mysterious work."[5]

If faith is the key it is also sometimes the problem because what we define as faith and what Pere de Caussade defines as faith may not always be the same thing. When John Main tells us to keep it simple, he knows there is a big difference between a simplicity of faith which is mature and a simplicity of faith which is immature. One allows God's love to flood the heart because the door to the heart is open; the other believes it has an adequate amount of love for the people and things it has chosen to love. The heart is firmly shut against the entry of any excess love.

Where people are deeply alienated from each other they are also alienated from God. The fact that such alienation is evident in a community which has centuries old paths worn to Christian churches says something about the immaturity of faith. That kind of faith has failed to build a love-centred community. The building blocks have been inadequate for the purpose.

Alexander Solzhenitsyn trying to account for the suffering inflicted on the twentieth century simply said "Men have forgotten God." It is not an easy accusation to face if you are a member of a Church. After all you believe in God, you pray to him, you play an active part in Church life and if asked you would say that He plays a central role in your life. How then can you or I be accused of forgetting him?

Another way of putting what Solzhenitsyn is saying is that we have forgotten who God is. There has been a blurring of his true identity. Somehow we have managed to put God in the wrong place. He is lost to us rather than forgotten by us. This is an important issue when we come to ask ourselves if we have made or can make the changes to our life and personality which the gospel demands. It forces us to look at where we have placed God among all the boxes and general jumble of our lives.

Everyone of us belongs to a group in some sense or another. We often belong to more than one group. We are loosely attached to some groups and passionately attached to others. Membership of groups can overlap. The same people turn up in group A and then in Group B. Sometimes the same people turn up so regularly that we begin to see them as not two groups at all but as one. The barrier that keeps them separate, that marks out the particular identity of each has become invisible. After a while the words "Group A" come to mean "Group B" and vice versa. While barriers of exclusivity can be unhealthy there are some barriers which are worth keeping in their place. There are dangers in moving from one group to the next. There may be characteristics of Group A which are true for that Group but are not at all true for Group B. The fact that so many members of Group A are also in Group B allows the ambiguity to arise. Sometimes though it is essential to challenge the ambiguity, to refuse to let it go unchallenged.

Take the terms Catholic and Protestant. It is perfectly reasonable to count faith in God as an element in both those terms for they are after all faith systems which cluster around Christ. Take the terms Nationalist and Unionist. These are political terms. People of all faiths and no faiths at all can adopt these labels and describe themselves as Nationalist or Unionist. The words Irish and British are terms which describe a persons ethnic origin or nationality. People of all faiths and no faith at all are equally entitled to use these labels. The word Ulster is a geographical term, used to describe a province of Ireland which encompasses nine counties of Ireland three in the South and six in the North.

Problems occur when we start to run these groupings together. Catholic, Nationalist, Irish. Three distinct groupings each with completely different functions and purposes find themselves collapsed into each other because so many of their members are the same. Since many people in Ireland are also Catholic how easy it is to move from the words Catholic and Ireland to that more loaded term "Catholic Ireland". How easy it is in turn, to move from that to an Ireland that God wants to be Catholic and Nationalist. The God at the core of Catholic faith and dogma suddenly becomes the God who is also on the side of Ireland and of nationalism. Isn't it amazing we tell ourselves that wherever we go, whatever we do, God is there too. But is he there as a gentle presence reconciling us to all humanity and to him? Or is he there as the superchampion of Catholic, Irish nationalism, the biggest, best and greenest of them all?

The same is true of the terms Protestant, British, and Unionist. God is jumped over the boxes. To be Protestant is to believe in God. To be Protestant is to be British. Therefore God must believe in being British. That makes God a Unionist. Simple isn't it? The battle cry goes up "For God and Ulster." Ulster is rounded down to the six counties of Northern Ireland and the ten commandments are rounded down to nine and a half. God is reduced to a weapon to beat our enemies with. Across the peace line people are really shouting, "My God is Bigger than your God. No he's not. My God is bigger than your God. Is! Isn't! Is! Isn't."

Careless use of words leads to a confused awareness of God. Instead of finding him alone and intimately as a friend, we bully him into a hundred campaigns of our choosing. He is the big boy we bring with us to fight the other big boys who have been picking on us. Looked at coldly this God looks familiar. And so he should for we have created him in our image and likeness. We have reversed roles. We are not the paper he writes on. He is the actor who speaks our script. Our God is as noisy, opinionated and bigoted as we are. He's on the peace line with a petrol bomb in his hand, a gun in his pocket, smiting and delivering thunderbolts like the God of the Old testament, as if Christ had never been born and had never spoken his words of reconciliation and peace.

How far is that flawed comprehension of God from the one described in these words by Dom Helder Camara?

> "What will you say?
> Look about you:
> from the stars in their millions in the heights
> to the stone, the water, to the animals, the plants,
> you walk
> among voiceless beings.
> Look about you again
> look
> until you see the invisible
> and you will tremble
> at the silence of the angels
> at the silence of God.
> Speak then..."[6]

He might also have said "act then".

There is a world of difference between opening ourselves to admit God on our own terms and conditions and opening ourselves to God unconditionally on his terms. When Helder Camara asks God to write the script, he walks out on the water in faith, he takes a risk for he agrees in advance to accept whatever the Lord writes. There can be no negotiation afterwards.

The Reconcilling Power of Silence

John Main says that

> "The proper ordering of our external activities can only be achieved once we have re-established conscious contact with the centre of all these activities and concerns. This centre is the aim of our meditation. It is the centre of our being. In St. Teresa's words, 'God is the centre of the soul.'"[7]

John Main shows how the path to this centre is achieved through silence and through meditative prayer. He acknowledges that meditation is not the only or exclusive path but it is one simple and universal way. Silence however, is not one of the things that we most value in the modern world. There are many reasons for the loss of this important spiritual value in daily life. Television for example, that used to fill a few hours in the day now fights silence round the clock. You can't have a tooth extracted, get your hair done or buy a bag of chips without music or chat shows invading your mental space.

We live in a world that has grown familiar with levels of noise and other forms of pollution which our grandparents would have found intolerable. We are sometimes so brainwashed by it that it is the absence of noisy distraction which disturbs us. Silence can be very disturbing when it confronts us with the true level of our own distraction and anxious self-obsession. The temptation then is to keep filling up with noise. I remember many years ago at a silent retreat making the awful mistake of choosing Rice Krispies for breakfast. Have you ever tried sucking Rice Krispies? When someone passed me a plate of crispy toast I almost disintegrated in panic. The silence was nerve-wracking. It still can be for me. Even now when I sit through silent meals at retreats or at a meditation centre part of me wants to shout and chatter. The silence is disturbing, conspiratorial. I don't want my own company at least not with all these people around. I want conviviality, banter, craic and conversation. I want to adapt to the pattern of the present world It is so much more comfortable at the moment, so much easier than learning what the attentiveness and poverty of silence feels like. No wonder John Main says "The problem is our distractedness, our possessiveness."

With a large family our home was always noisy. The minute it got quiet my mother got suspicious. Quiet, meant that all hell was shortly about to break loose. But there was a quiet time just after all the kids had gone to school and my father had returned from the school run with fresh scones from the bakery just for the two of them. On the rare mornings when I was ill in bed and the house was empty,I relished that special intimate silence when I had my mother and father all to myself. You could feel the relationships assume a different kind of ease born of the shared silence, the peace, the lack of doing, the period of just being. Those were the hours when I felt I most belonged to these two people, when I could almost touch the spirit which bound us to each other through birth. There was a wonder at the discovery that there actually were parts of the day when you did not have to be busy.

Today we manage to teach children busyness and pressure from an early age. Life is all go, from the mad rush for the bathroom, the hasty breakfast, the gallop to the school bus, the school day itself segmented into periods of activity. Periods of silence are rare and usually accidental. Little space for silence is woven into children's lives. They hardly know what to do with silence when it suddenly descends.

I feel privileged that as a child I had those quiet hours with my mother and father. I also had the privilege of often sitting in the stillness of a darkened church with my grandmother who had consciously made space for silence in her life and was marvellously energised by it. When she sat there praying in that blessed stillness she was looking inward at the incomprehensibility of God, drawing meaning from within. Looked at from outside, her life was all drudgery and hardship. To an outsider her life would have been remarkable only for its lack of fulfilment, its constant battle with despair and with the vacuum of loneliness which assailed her when her children scattered through emigration to the corners of the earth.

As John Main neatly put it "Every pattern we try to impose on our experience from outside inevitably falsifies the truth." My grandmother carved her own truth in those daily silences when she dedicated her life anew to God's love, handed it over to his work and reconciled herself to whatever was written on the blank sheet of her life. It conferred on her a dignity and a self-possessedness which came from the assurance that there was after all a God who truly loved her. No matter what she had or lacked, no matter how she looked, no matter what she brought to those morning meetings in the cold and in the dark silence of a country church, she felt infinitely valued in the love of God. If she was a saint as many who knew her said she was then it probably helped greatly in her marriage to my grandfather. She certainly fulfiled the observation that a saint is what it takes to be married to a martyr. He was a deeply religious man but a strong adherent of the school of lamentation and martyrdom. The world was always miserable for him.He was the sole martyr who had to put up with it. He was afflicted especially by the fact that his son, my father had gone off to the 'black North,' married there and had children whose credentials as Catholics would always be suspect because of their proximity to those of the other persuasion.

"I don't suppose you say the Family Rosary at all up there" he once remarked. We defended our home valiantly, lying that of course we said the Rosary every night. "Right so," he conceded,

"You can give out the Litany at the end." This was one of those occasions where you wanted God to punish you straight away with death. A bolt of lightning before we got to the Litany of the Blessed Virgin was needed to prevent our exposure and save our family's reputation. Once we had started the litany I could get no further than "Mirror of Justice". My sister God Bless her, came to the rescue. Leaning towards his deaf ear she took up where I left off.

"Church of England" she added firmly.

"Pray for us" he replied unperturbed.

"Church of Ireland.... Church of Scotland." she continued and when she ran out of churches she took up bingo calls; "Two little ducks. Legs eleven." He prayed happily for them all. We survived.

There is another approach to prayer in the contemplative dimension, very different from my grandfather's litany and offering an experience of God as mystery rather than compulsive certainty. "Prayer" says John Main "means being absolutely still, absolutely silent before the incomprehensibility of God." To the person who is already sure he knows everything God is not mysterious. What is mysterious to them are other people's queer views of God!

Out of the mysteriousness of God there emerges a new experience of divine compassion. Joseph Goldstein, a Buddhist teacher of meditation, says

> *"Over a period of time, meditation develops a tremendous*
> *tenderness of heart .... a softening of the mind and heart*
> *takes place that transforms the way we relate to ourselves*
> *and to others. We begin to feel more deeply and this depth*
> *of feeling becomes the well-spring of compassion."*[8]

This could have been written of my grandmother, a woman of profound and generous compassion. Her heart was soft, softened by the silent prayer around which her life revolved. Between herself and my grandfather there was a kind of peace wall of the heart and mind, over which periodically he threw his miseries and she corralled her disappointments. But that wall too was permeable and her silent prayer was her way of bringing reconciliation to her home. Once when we children were leaving her after a holiday spent at the cottage, I felt a deep pity for her now that all our fun and laughter was leaving too. I said that I hoped she wouldn't be too lonely with just the two of them. "Arrah" she said "Don't be worrying, sure there's the three of us in it. Himself, Meself and the Good Lord." A woman reconciled to suffering without bitterness and radiant with a love that made unavoidable hardships bearable.

FOOTNOTES CHAPTER 5.

1   Romans 12: 1-2
2   "Holidays in Hell" by P.J.O'Rourke, pub. Picador 1989
3   per Redmond Fitzmaurice in "Sectarianism" A Discussion Document, Irish Inter-Church Meeting 1993
4   "A Thousand Reasons for Living" by Dom Helder Camara, quoted in "Interpreted by Love, An Anthology of Praise" by Elizabeth Bassett, Darton, Longmand and Todd 1994
5   "Sacrament of the Present Moment" by Jean-Pierre de Caussade, pub. Fount Paperbacks 1996
6   Dom Helder Camara, op.cit.
7   "The Inner Christ", by John Main, pub. Darton, Longman and Todd, 1987
8   "Insight Meditation, The Practice of Freedom" by Joseph Goldstein, pub. Shambhala, 1993

6

BUILDING A RECONCILED WORLD

The Croatian theologian Miroslav Wolf faced a dilemma familiar to many of us in Ireland, and other countries experiencing ethnic conflict. His country was tearing itself apart, fracturing along ethnic and cultural faultlines. Typical of any conflict, each side saw itself as the only wounded victim, and "the other" as oppressor exactly as in Northern Ireland. Locked into the vanity and absurdity of its own martyrdom complex, each waited in vain for the other to apologise. It was a time to stand up and be counted but with whom? In the resulting stalemate, believing his culture to be estranged from God, he asked where do Christians fit in; how do they relate to such a situation?

Wolf talks tough about the Christian responsibility for reconciliation:

> "The root of Christian self-understanding... lies in the destiny of Jesus Christ, his mission and his rejection which ultimately brought him to the Cross. 'He came to what was his own and his own people did not accept him' (John 1: 11) He was a stranger to the world because the world into which he came was estranged from God... It is therefore not a matter of indifference for Christians whether or not to be 'strangers' in their own culture; to the extent that one's own culture has been estranged from God, distance from it is essential to Christian identity".[1]

What is important to understand about this estrangement is that we are called to be strangers, prophetic voices, voices of contradiction from within our own cultures not from outside them. We are to be distanced and estranged but we are not to be outsiders who have abandoned our own or run away from them in order to set up another exclusive world, a safe haven. As Wolf says, "Distance from a culture must never degenerate into a flight from that culture."[2] This is still my culture, my country, my denomination, my community, my family but I do not have to swallow whole and in stoical silence, its wrong-headedness, its pigheadedness, or its madness. My Christianity has to shape my perspective on this place I inhabit and on these people with whom I cohabit. I know through that sharing of life and place with others, that God is creating a new world, a world in which every man, woman and child, past present and to come, every nation, language creed and race will be reconciled in him. The Christian knows, that eventually, all will be reconciled in love. If I imagine for one moment that this new world will come when everyone has thrown in the towel and become an Irish Catholic, or an Ulster Protestant, then I have badly missed his point. Wolf believes that 'Christians take a distance from their own culture because they give the ultimate allegiance to God and God's future'.

It is that distance which allows us to cast a loving but critical eye over what happens around us and in our name. It enables us to distinguish truth from lies, injustice from justice, the important from the unimportant. But as he says,

> "In situations of ethnic conflict churches often find themselves accomplices in war rather than agents of peace. We find it difficult to distance ourselves from our own culture and so we echo its reigning opinions and mimic its practices. As we keep the vision of God's future alive, we need to reach out across the firing lines and join hands with our brothers and sisters on the other side. We need to let them pull us out of the enclosure of our own culture and its own peculiar set of prejudices so that we can read afresh 'the one Word of God'"[3]

Christian life has become corrupted by a chronic failure to

establish and maintain the distance which reconciliation requires. This failure runs through the history of Christianity just as it pockmarks our own contemporary world. Too often it seems we Christians only hurt when "our side" is hurt; the only pain we feel and acknowledge is our own. Our immediate sense of time and space, our close allegiance to the politics of the present moment often blocks our understanding of the need for this sense of distance and detachment. When we say "Thy Kingdom come", it is worth asking ourselves, 'What is our timeframe? What is God's?'

A Sense of History

On a visit to a dinosaur exhibition with my children I was struck by the length of the dinosaur's dynasty on this planet. They were around for 160 million years. It puts a mere two thousand years of Christianity into perspective. If the Lord was sitting up in heaven watching a long video of edited highlights of life on earth from the beginning of time, all of humanity would flash past in a split second. The Lord would be watching an awful lot of dinosaurs. It is worth reminding ourselves how long He took to get very bored with dinosaurs!

In his famous essay on the interior life, 'Le Milieu Divin' Teilhard de Chardin paints an image of a God who is getting on with his work through the long centuries, who is salvaging the good from all we do, sifting out the evil, and whose pace is so steady but slow, that we, in our impatience fail to see or recognise his kingdom is coming all around us. This is a difficult but a beautiful piece of spiritual writing, probably the most beautiful and prophetic in this century:

> "We are sometimes inclined to think that the same things
> are monotonously repeated over and over again in the
> history of creation. That is because the season is too long by
> comparison with the brevity of our individual lives, and the

transformation too vast and too inward by comparison with our superficial and restricted outlook, for us to see the progress of what is tirelessly taking place in and through all matter and spirit. Let us believe in revelation, once again our faithful support in our most human forebodings. Under the commonplace envelope of things and of all our purified and salvaged efforts, a new earth is being slowly engendered.

"One day, the Gospel tells us, the tension gradually accumulating between humanity and God will touch the limits prescribed by the possibilities of the world. And then will come the end. The presence of Christ, which has been silently accruing in things, will suddenly be revealed- like a flash of light from pole to pole. Breaking through all the barriers within which the veil of matter and the water-tightness of souls have seemingly kept it confined, it will invade the face of the earth... Like lightning, like a conflagration, like a flood, the attraction exerted by the Son of Man will lay hold of all the whirling elements in the universe so as to reunite them or subject them to his body... As the Gospel warns us, it would be in vain to speculate as to the hour and the modalities of this formidable event. But we have to expect it... that is perhaps the supreme Christian function and the most distinctive characteristic of our religion... The Lord Jesus will only come soon if we ardently expect him... successors to Israel, we Christians have been charged with keeping the flame of desire ever alive in the world. Only twenty centuries have passed since the Ascension. What have we made of our expectancy?

"A rather childish haste, combined with the error in perspective which led the first generation of Christians to believe in the immediate return of Christ, has unfortunately left us disillusioned and suspicious. Our faith

in the Kingdom of God has been disconcerted by the
resistance of the world to good. A certain pessimism has
encouraged us... to regard the world as decidedly and
incorrigibly wicked. And so we have allowed the flame to
die down in our sleeping hearts... in reality we should have
to admit, if we were sincere that we no longer expect
anything."[4]

Coming out of the ignominy of the World War Two, the
Holocaust and Hiroshima it is not difficult to see why people
should no longer expect anything good of the world. In fact they
often steel themselves to expect the worst. There is little peace in
knowing that humanity now has the power to take on God. We can
reduce the earth, our part of creation at least, to ashes if we have a
mind to. We can even do it in the name of God, or Allah. After all,
one of the holiest of shrines, the birthplace of Christ himself, is
ravaged by an ethno/religious war of the grimmest savagery.

Reassurance and revelation, however, persist in reaching us in
peculiar ways. A man emerges from four years of savage captivity in
Beirut and speaks a language that is vaguely but deeply familiar. It
attests to the existence of a loving presence which embraces all
humankind. He won't call it God, why should he, he has seen what
Gods can do on the streets of Belfast and this is of a different order
of magnitude altogether. But we can acknowledge it as one of those
times when the presence of love reveals itself powerfully,
convincingly and reassuringly.

An elderly black man emerges from a quarter century of
captivity in South Africa, into a country in racial foment, a powder
keg ready to blow. It looks like a straight fight between the God of
White supremacy and the God of Black liberation. The latter have
the numbers, the former have the weapons. Instead when
Archbishop Desmond Tutu shouts 'Yippee!' and dances in the
streets we know this is not a dance of black triumphalism but a
surge of joy in celebration of a victory for a god of love. South Africa
struggles to build on the foundation of an embrace between

oppressor and oppressed. It is not easy and it is not yet stable but intuitively we know that what is happening is right; it is the unfolding of God's plan for his world.

The Christian church faces a crisis of vocations as its traditional male clerical system of power and privilege disintegrates under its own dead-weight. Women come forward to say they have vocations and they want to be allowed to respond to God's call. This flood of new gifts is embraced in nervous dribs and drabs by most though clearly not all of the Christian churches. God rubs the revelation right under their noses. Many predictably see the newly-won dignity of women in the same way that the people of Jerusalem saw Christ: as an upstart, a pain in the neck – they wish it would go away and give them peace but the many start to look like the fewer and fewer!

Men committed to violence as a means of addressing political and social oppression agree to silence their weapons and engage in talk. They have committed themselves to a process of conversion. These are blessed happenings, not gifts to be thrown back at God because we do not like the wrapping, or the messenger who brings them. And every life will have its own commentary to give on all the other signs in the modern world which sharply remind us of God's nearness. It is not an easy world in which to articulate those signs of our own times. Ours is not the first time or culture to have grown impatient with and dismissive of God. Ours is the first however in which the reach of cynicism is so global and so strong.

It is easy to become disheartened and doubt-ridden in the power of faith to bring about reconciliation when religious sensibilities are so regularly the butt of cynicism and are repudiated without fair hearing. Much of the criticism directed against organised religion may well be deserved change, but much of it is lazy, trite and no more than secular bigotry. The once automatic deference which was given to Churches, ministers, Christian dogma and the symbols of faith has virtually disappeared. In its place are a range of responses extending from complete indifference to a crass in-your-face sneering irreverence. Every minor or major peccadillo of a Christian politician or priest is held up to a harsh light, and inevitably found deficient. Both he and church are promptly condemned and consigned with delicious delight to the bin of oblivion. A media which feeds on scandal, can feed doubt and undermine our commitment. Belief in God and membership of a denomination are regularly portrayed as signs of intellectual weakness or fundamentalist tendencies. The intolerant and unjust can throw the most vehement accusations of intolerance and injustice against others without themselves ever being called to account.

Adding to our uncertainties for the future are those fears and doubts which are being generated from within the denominational boundaries. Ecumenical dialogue has softened the denominational boundaries which used to be so transparent and so important. But even that once enthusiastic and pioneering dialogue now blows hot and cold often sending mixed and inconsistent messages. There is a feeling that identities are not quite as focused as they used to be inside the old denominational boundaries. The edges where we interface with other religions are also blurred particularly if you view that interface with fear and doubt. Dialogue is frequently, if privately, regarded by religious leaders as the first step towards the betrayal of one's own identity. We are not so confident or so clear as we once were about where the tide of change is leading. Twenty years ago, for example, the ship of change in the Roman Catholic Church had a strong confident wind behind it as the impact of Vatican II kicked in. Now it seems becalmed or even pulled backwards away from renewal. Often one senses a tiredness among ordinary believers, a why-should-we bother-any more attitude as if they have lost faith in the process and the objective, as if de Chardin's words warning of the dying of the flame of faith are proving true.

Yet there is rich irony in that tiredness because it occurs at just that point in the spiritual history of the world when things are beginning to get really exciting, perhaps as exciting as they have been since the First coming of Christ two thousand years ago. What are the grounds for this millennial hope?

Global communication networks have created sophisticated and rapid vehicles for information handling of every conceivable variety. Radio, television, newspapers, journals, books, e-mail, world wide web, satellites, airplanes, cars, all park us on the cusp of a communications and access revolution which makes the early adventures of Columbus look like a day trip to the zoo. The sheer reach of our communications is even more exciting than its technical brilliance. The concept of oneness in diversity, and particularly in diversity, is not difficult to explain. Cultures open up to each other. They share food, music, poetry, spirituality and tacky ethnic gifts. We eat Chinese food, wear Italian shoes, go to Thailand on holidays, use American slang, worry about South American rain forests, try to adopt Romanian babies. Our own personal experiential boundaries are shifting at an amazing pace.

An explosion of education has wrestled the ownership of knowledge from the privileged few to the masses. Where before we had only one version of 'the truth', we now have many challenging and contradicting each other. Where history was once largely HIS story it is now being balanced with HER story. Voices which were once silent or silenced have now come in from the margins to centre stage to tell their story and to stake their claim to intellectual space. Things which were once hidden and taboo are now brought to the surface and dealt with, whether it is child sex abuse dating back to the 1950's, or self-serving collaboration with Nazism by international banks, whether it is political corruption by political leaders or moral corruption by spiritual leaders. Investigative journalism, crass tabloidism, the relentless pursuit of the long range lens, organisations like Childline have narrowed the scope for hypocrisy and shortened the odds that the truth will out. There are those who see every church-based scandal as just another nail in the Church's coffin. Others see in all this the incorrigible wickedness that de Chardin warned of. Both views, I feel, fail to see in these signs some of the much deeper and hope-filled responses which are being awakened and empowering people world-wide. On the other side of the gloom, there is the increasingly widespread demand for greater authenticity in living out the gospel, and a refusal to accept that which is mere sham. There is also a call for repentance, for a change of ways and forgiveness based on truth not denial.

These are ultimately healthy developments though the subject matter they bring up from the silence is often shocking and horrifying. We are learning painfully the human cost of these silences, the lives distorted and warped by abuse, as skewed childhoods give way to tortured adulthoods. The humbling effect of many of these scandals on those who would otherwise be the voices of authority in the institutions which are under scrutiny has had an interesting downstream consequence. New voices are speaking confidently, asserting their right to be heard. As in many crises the weak prove their strength and the strong are embarrassed by their weakness. Those who thought they were the teachers have become the pupils. Both see each other through new eyes. We grow wiser. Some grow harder. Some grow cold to Christ. Their anger and their indignation are understandable. The role of those who remain committed to Christ is to keep trying to strive for the authenticity of vision which will re-inspire the despairing and once again produce the green shoots of belief in barren places.

Stories, New Hopes

Old stories just won't do any more. If they are based on lies sooner or later they will be exposed. The syrupy hagiographies of the powerful and famous which we were once fed and which encouraged imitative, unreal lives will not wipe the jaundiced eyes of this or the next generation. Big institutions once deemed arrogant and unassailable have had to apologise in public for the mistakes and chaos they have kept hidden.

There is a precious liberation in being able to admit the things we did wrong, whether personally, institutionally, nationally, historically. We are ultimately relieved to discover that we can acknowledge our failures candidly. We do not have to bury the dark leprous side of our world and its past. We can prepare young people for a world in which human beings inevitably stumble, fall, pick themselves up and try again. We can equip them with an understanding of the essentially courageous humanity we possess but also the essentially flawed humanity we all share. Most important of all we can teach young people that the Christian gospel imposes on us an obligation to reconcile belief and action, to fuse form and substance, to strive to live life in his love and to keep on trying when we fail. That teaching mission is essential at a time when the litany of failures of Christians whether at the level of the personal, institutional or cultural, has often created a response close to "been there, done that, didn't work, forget it".

What draws many of us to John Main as a teacher is both the freshness and the fixedness of his focus, his insistence on keeping to this teaching agenda, the sheer relentlessness of his pursuit of reconciliation with Christ. His belief in the perennial newness of Christ shows us that the worst way of adapting to the multiplicity of crises around us is to descend into lamentation – as if the first coming had never happened and the second coming had not been promised. Yet this lamentation characterises so much of our social discourse today. What, de Chardin, once asked, have we done with our sense of expectancy?

We need to ask ourselves the same question today. Where is the perennial newness of our Christian hope, the newness assured by the Resurrection? What partnerships will we forge, comfortable or uncomfortable with the new generation of movers and shakers, ideas generators whether on this island and on the neighbouring island and elsewhere on earth? It is a question which affects the future of all work for reconciliation and the Church's role in the process both on the island of Ireland as well as in the rest of the world. Have we even begun to imagine the synergies which could be unleashed if we could make the new, life-renewing connections which are disclosed by every courageously pursued process of reconciliation?

As the Abbe de Tourville says,

> *"Intelligent people can no longer deceive themselves about old systems and old ideas, circumstances have radically changed and changed beyond possibility of recall... Be open to new ideas and be glad to put them into practice."*[5]

If some of our old certainties have passed their sell-by dates what new ideas are we prepared to flirt with? Could Ireland with its living history of conflict and violence help to show the world the way? Can a deep faith and hope in the reality of reconciliation set us on course for an as yet unscripted new set of relationships between Ireland, North and South, and Great Britain? Is there an embrace which can underscore the fundamental bond of affection between British and Irish, Catholic and Protestant, which can sideline the historic enmities and maintain boundaries of difference which are respected and celebrated rather than feared and threatened. Are the Christian churches and the Christians in them prepared to play a prophetic role in redeeming not just these islands but themselves?

Who would not be thankful for a chance to succeed at something we once failed in? Now that chance is here, do we recognise it as ours? Are we so overwhelmed by the scale of our previous failure that we are paralysed? Or are we only sure that the time is ripe for change provided that "the other" changes first? This is the hour we are called into the garden of Gethsemani. The spotlight is on us. What are we going to do with our expectancy? What sign will we be?

My grandfather's grave is marked by a granite headstone on which the date is incorrectly carved. We asked if it could be fixed. The answer was no. What was written was written forever, engraved on stone. The only sure answer to the problem was to replace the headstone with a new one. A fresh new piece of granite on which to chisel a new script. If only political problems, the results of so many past mistakes, were as easily solved.

In the verbal crossfire which will now take the place of violence in Northern Ireland will we hear mere recitals of old hurts, old litanies and warcries? Or will we hear a new language, conveying new ideas, capable of chiselling a new script? How can we ensure that this process on which our future peace and prosperity rests is dedicated to the building up of God's future as well as our own? de Chardin says "Nothing is more certain than that human action can be sanctified". He meant that quite literally. He was not talking about certain types of human action like praying, fasting and giving to charity but rather "the whole of human life down to its most natural zones". "Whether you eat or drink", as St. Paul says. Every act could and should be done in a "spirit of adoration". He meant acts of individuals and acts of conglomerates, acts done by one individual and acts done in the name of all. Even the acts and words of politicians and those who support them! de Chardin had a prayer which could inspire anyone, from any tradition, on any side, in any conflict, with the confidence to achieve reconciliation.

> *"May the time come when men (and women) having been awakened to the close bond linking all the movements of this world in the single all-embracing work of the Incarnation, shall be unable to give themselves to any one of their tasks without illuminating it with the clear vision that their work, however elementary it may be, is received and put to good use by a Centre of the Universe."*[6]

In the work of peace every little counts.

FOOTNOTES CHAPTER 6.

1   "A Vision of Embrace, Theological Perspectives on Cultural Identity and Conflict" by Miroslav Wolf

2,3 ibid

4   "Le Milieu Divin" by Teilhard de Chardin, pub. Collins Fontana Books 1957

5   "Letters of Direction" by Abbe de Tourville

6   de Chardin op.cit.

THE MINISTRY OF RECONCILIATION

Reconciliation involves finding new language for, and new ways of seeing, familiar situations. In Ireland, for example, the work of reconciliation means that those churches which are embedded in the conflict must be unshackled from the chains which bind them to the language of conflict. Their language has to become the word of God and not a version of the word of God which has been selectively edited and conveniently paraphrased so that it matches exactly our political and cultural ambitions. The only way to be sure we are listening to and actually hearing the true word of God is to place ourselves in an environment where our version of God's word is exposed to other versions and where we are challenged and can challenge in turn.

No one is being asked to surrender their denomination in this reconciling work of mutual listening. What can there really be to fear in merely meeting, merely listening to the other? Are we so fearful of the vulnerability of our belief that we expect it will crumble when exposed to the scrutiny of others? Have we no confidence in the durability of the dogmas that we are protecting? Can they not survive exposure to air? And if they cannot what does it say of their value in the first place? Can we say we are honouring the commandment to love one another if we refuse even to listen to the other? If we presume that we alone know the mind of God have we not ceased to be his friend and become instead his self-appointed sole agent?

The concept of God's Church as family is, I believe, the key. That image of family is robust enough to accommodate many sub-divisions each with its own veracity and its own integrity.

I am a member of a family of nine brothers and sisters each of whom has left home and formed new subdivisions each a new family in its own right. We are still family to each other but we will never live again under the same roof (if we can possibly avoid it). Asked to describe our mother and father we would each have quite different perspectives. Each description has its own truth but to compare one with the other will throw up contradictions and create ambiguities. Put all nine together and you will get some sense of the persons our parents are but the pictures will still be incomplete. Their friends and brothers and sisters will want their say too and when their pen pictures are added in we look as if these two people have personalities split enough to keep three Jungian psycho-analysts busy for years. One thing we will say is that they loved their children. After that it is a free for all.

I may be happy to live without ever knowing what my brothers or sisters' views of my parents are but I would be very wrong to presume that my view is also their view. In seeking to understand their views I am not wanting to take anything from them but rather to enhance my comprehension of the whole world my parents inhabited and not just the bit I was comfortable in. The fact that we have quite different experiences and memories has come back to me many times as I have explained to my younger siblings, who do not remember, the impact on our lives of particular incidents like losing our home and business through sectarian violence. I have memories and understandings they do not share. Every so often we need to remind each other of that truth. We need to be patient too with the gaps in each other's understanding. There is a lot of catching up to do.

What is true of us as individuals in a family is true of the churches generally. Each has its own memory of revelation, its own perspective on God. They have much to share with each other. The decision to learn from each other, however, is entirely separate from the decision to listen to each other. The embrace of reconciliation may be no more than inviting the stranger into our house to look without prejudice, to take us as they find us. Or it may be a real sharing like that which occurred when the Hindu swami Satyananda invited the Christian John Main to benefit from his insight into meditation.

As we pick up speed towards the millennium many are already becoming bored with the hype of millenniumitis, all the count downs and expensive parties planned. The emphasis has, to put it mildly, been less than spiritual. There are the soothsayers and doomsellers who hawk apocalyptic rantings around in the name of a God whom they have personally talked to; but there has been little attention given to the spiritual significance and opportunity of this anniversary. It is helpful to reflect on what the millennium truly marks. It is nothing less than the Great Jubilee of Christendom as Pope John Paul II has reminded us. And yet, when the clock turns and all the zeroes click into place where will all the Christian churches be turned to at that moment? What will the rest of the world notice about them? Will the churches have invited each other to their parties or will their affairs be strictly private? Will they enter this coming new millennium as true friends or virtual strangers? Will they have invited their non-Christian co-believers to come and watch? Will they have established their relevance at all?

Will the great divides be as wide after the party as before? Christian churches to date have abysmally failed to convincingly capture this jubilee celebration and claim it as theirs. Consequently they have also failed to connect the celebration to the person of Christ, Pope John Paul's apostolic letter *Tertio Millennio Adveniente* notwithstanding. It is as if we are the children of parents approaching their fiftieth wedding anniversary. It should be a great celebration but this was a miserable marriage and there is not much stomach for a big celebration. It would be an exercise in hypocrisy. The children play the whole thing down in their embarrassment. The great gift to the children would be if the parents gave real leadership even at this late hour. It is not too late to bury hatchets, and repair bridges, to embrace, "the other" but time is running out. This precious moment of opportunity for a major act of reconciliation will not be repeated. Once gone it cannot be recaptured.

The historian Arnold Toynbee has predicted that a new religious consciousness will emerge through a realignment between Buddhism and Christianity. The possibilities of such an embrace are fascinating even awesome. The mere hint of it, however, will have many racing for the sandbags to reinforce the barricades. But in the context of a world that must prepare for Christ's second coming what other path is there for us all to travel if it is not the path to each other?

If we are honest we can admit that the Christian churches approaching the millennium are in poor enough shape. Those of us on the inside know there is also vibrancy and renewal but we also know there is a bewildering sense of loss and of barrenness which characterises Christianity for so many today. Those of us born into inherited faith systems which we have subsequently chosen to claim as our own are deeply saddened and disturbed by the prospect of a dying Church. Our sadness though is, alleviated and ultimately overcome by hope. It is the hope inherent in faith: the hope that finds soil in which to grow and ripen.

Lorca writes beautifully of the despair of the barren in his description of the plight of the Withered Orange Tree:

> *Woodcutter, Cut my shadow. Deliver me from the torture of beholding myself fruitless.*
> *Why was I born surrounded by mirrors? The day turns round me. And the night reproduces me in each of her stars.*
> *I want to live without seeing myself. And I shall dream that ants and hawks are my leaves and birds.*
> *Woodcutter, Cut my shadow. Deliver me from this torture of beholding myself fruitless.*[1]

This could be the cry of many people of faith who are deeply unsure that the baton of belief and hope has been safely handed onto the next generation.

The Role of the Reconcilers

Sometimes signs can be deceptive. When I renovated my grand-father's cottage a few years ago I planted a special tree in the front garden to mark the new life that was beginning there. It flourished for two years but one weekend I returned after a stormy night to find it had broken in two. We intended to remove the stump but did not find time to do it until we returned to the house the following spring. We were amazed to find that around the bottom of the stump vigorous new growth had appeared and the tree is today stronger, healthier than it ever was.

All around us, if we look carefully enough, we will see signs of vigorous new growth. The clearest of all signs are human beings themselves. As the Abbe de Tourville said,

> 'God has scattered forerunners in the world. They are those who are ahead of their time and whose personal action is based on an inward knowledge of that which is to come...'[2]

Among these signs of hope, these forerunners of a new era, are people like Thomas Merton, Bede Griffiths, and John Main, Mother Teresa, who have pointed the way to a future where the oneness of God can be richly acknowledged in the midst of the diversity of religions and cultures. As Dom Bede Griffiths has said,

> 'To me the meeting of Western religions with the religions of the East is really one of the focal points of human development today. I do not feel that religions can go on simply following their own path separately. We have reached a point in evolution where we have to meet. We have to share, to discover one another.'[3]

His words are reflected by John Main in the Inner Christ:

> 'There is a need for men and women who are not religious bigots, not intolerant of other religious men and women but who are strong with the power of the Spirit and who know

that it is a universal spirit of love. We need Christian people
who realise that we have nothing to fear from the Buddhist
tradition or the Hindu tradition or any tradition that is
truly spiritual.'[4]

A wit once remarked that religion is for those who want to get
to heaven. Spirituality is for those who are coming from hell. It does
not have to be a choice between one or other. Religion without
spirituality is already hell. At its most unredeemed it can keep hell
going. In Northern Ireland the ruthless alliance of religion without
spirituality and politics are so powerful that it can obliterate the
very humanity and loveability of people of the 'other'. Together
they can drown out the commandment to love. In the Churches,
dogmatic theology, dogmatically adhered to, can drown out the
voice of revelation. In both the religious and social spheres, we are
consequently impoverished because the arteries of grace become
clogged up. We always get a trickle through but we are denied the
full flood.

John Main once remarked to a friend that he felt he was playing
a role most of the time. The idea is not just a throw away line. It has
a strong positive meaning. When we take on the mantle of Christ
we are called to play a role in some theatre of life, on our own
particular stage. He gives us the script. He selects us for the part. As
Main said to his family when they expressed surprise at his decision
to leave law lecturing and become a Benedictine monk – "It isn't
that I want to, it's that I must."

These are days for deciding what it is we must do, not what we
want to do. The role we play in God's work of reconciling the world
to himself is our destiny. To find it and embrace it as John Main did
is our path to happiness. He has much to teach us still. A man
before his time he was offended by his church's misogyny and knew
it was insidiously disfiguring Christ's image. He was inspired by the
Spirit's renewal of his church because he knew it needed to be
renewed if it was to communicate the gospel effectively. He
believed that in the spiritual depth of meditation people from all

walks of life could discover their extraordinary vocation, their vocation as friends of Christ.

John Main is a sign of hope for a world struggling its way towards reconciliation. He is a special sign of hope for Ireland. He was a quintessential Irishman born in England and a quintessential Englishman who lived in Ireland. He reconciled love for many cultures and religions without ever abandoning his own faith or his own culture. He opened his own church up to the prayer experience of the eastern religions and in so doing rediscovered the contemplative riches of his own tradition. His inner journey took him to strange places as the journey to reconciliation, with ourselves, with others and with God, will generally do. It took him into profound self-knowledge, beyond the narrow pettiness of the ego, and its conflicts. From the self it led him into the presence and the mind of Christ and to an all-embracing vision of loving embrace for all humanity.

It was a risky journey which he undertook in faith. But he had a guide whom he knew he could trust. The guide was all he needed. Commanded by the guide to love, he did so, discovering in each act of love and reconciliation the authenticity and sureness of his guide's wisdom. Long long before, his guide had reconciled the world to God through his own death on the cross. Reconciliation is not a meeting of strangers but a recognition of friends, a lesson we only learn when we take the first tentative steps towards "the other" and realise we were after all simply waiting for each others embrace.

FOOTNOTES CHAPTER 7.

1   "Cancion Del Naranjo Seco" from "Selected Poems", by
    Lorca pub. Penguin Books 1960
2   "Letters of Direction" by Abbe de Tourville
3   "The Marriage of East and West" by Bede Griffiths, pub.
    Collins Fount 1983
4   "The Inner Christ" by John Main, pub. Darton, Longman
    and Todd 1987

JOHN MAIN

John Main was born in London in 1926 into an Irish family. He studied law, learned Chinese and then served in the British Foreign Service in Malaya. There he was introduced to meditation by an Indian monk. At that time silent, non-conceptual prayer was rare and unfamiliar for most Christians. The long-standing Christian contemplative tradition had bee forgotten and replaced largely with 'mental prayer' and ritual. After his service in the East, John Main returned to Europe where he continued his meditation practice as the foundation of his Christian life. He became a Professor of international law at Trinity College, Dublin.

John Main became a Benedictine monk in 1958 in London and was advised to stop meditating as the practice was not deemed to be part of the Christian tradition of prayer. But in 1969 he rediscovered a Christian tradition of meditation or 'pure prayer' as it was called. This early form of meditation was taught by the Desert Fathers, the first Christian monks, to St Benedict and the Western church.

Having returned to his practice of meditation, John Main then dedicated the rest of his life to teaching this lost tradition of Christian prayer to lay people of all ages and walks of life. He believed it was important for the world to restore a spiritual practice of depth to people's ordinary lives. He recommended two periods of meditation, each morning and evening, which could also be integrated, with other forms of prayer.

John Main died in 1982. His work and vision is continued by a growing world-wide network of Christian meditation groups and centres. The International Centre of The World Community for Christian Meditation organises an annual Seminar in John Main's honour.

The John Main Seminar 1984 –1997

1984 Isabelle Glover: Indian Scriptures as Christian Reading

1985 Robert Kiely: The Search for God in Modern Literature

1986 John Todd: The New Church

1987 Charles Taylor: Christian Identity and Modernity

1988 Balfour Mount: On Wholeness

1989 Derek Smith : On Reading

1990 Eileen O'Hea:: Psyche and Spirit

1991 Bede Griffiths: Christian Meditation: An Evolving Tradition

1992 Jean Vanier: From Brokenness to Wholeness

1993 William Johnston: The New Christian Mysticism

1994 The Dalai Lama: The Good Heart

1995 Laurence Freeman: On Jesus

1996 Raimon Panikkar: The Silence of Life

1997 Mary McAleese: Reconciled Being

The World Community for Christian Meditation

Meditation creates community. Since the first Christian Meditation Centre was started by John Main in 1975 a steadily growing community of Christian meditators has spread around the world. Individual meditators frequently meet in small weekly groups and the network of these groups provides wider support and encouragement for people who wish to sustain their daily practice of morning and evening meditation.

The groups spread through more than a hundred countries meet in homes, parishes, schools, prisons, business, communities, government departments and hospitals. Many

Christian Meditation Centres some residential also serve to communicate the way of silence and stillness taught in this tradition

The International Centre in London co-ordinates this worldwide family of meditators. A quarterly newsletter giving spiritual teaching and reflection is sent out from London and also disseminates local and international news of retreats and other events being held in the Community. The centre is funded entirely by donations, especially through the Friends Programme. To contact a Christian Meditation group or Centre near you, please contact us at

International Centre,
The World Community for Christian Meditation,
23 Kensington Square,
London W8 5HN
United Kingdom
Tel: 0171 937 4679
Fax:0171 937 6790
Email:WCCM@Compuserve.com

The Web Page Address of the Community is
HYPERLINK http://www.wccm.org

In Ireland:

Christian Meditation Centre	Christian Meditation Centre
58 Meadow Grove	4 Eblana Avenue
Blackrock,	Dun Laoghaire,
Co. Cork	Co. Dublin
Tel: 021 357 249	Tel: 01 280 1505

Medio
Media

MEDIO MEDIA

Medio Media is the publishing arm of the World Community for Christian Meditation. It is committed to the dissemination of the teaching of meditation in the Christian tradition and in particular to the work of John Main. It is further committed to the growing dialogue among meditators and seekers from all traditions based on the deeper experience of silence shared by all religions.

A catalogue of Medio Media's publications – books, audio sets and videos – is available from:

Medio Media
23 Kensington Square, London W8 5HN, United Kingdom
Tel: 0171 937 4679
Fax: 0171 937 6790
E:Mail: wccm@compuserve.com

Also published by Medio Media in association with Arthur James:

The On Retreat With... Series

This new series responds to the spiritual needs of people living today's busy and stressed lifestyles. Each book in the series is designed to allow the reader to develop a space for silence and solitude and spiritual practice in the context of daily life or by taking a short period of withdrawal – 'do-it-yourself' retreat. The structure of the book allows a flexible timetable to be constructed which integrates periods of reading, physical practice or exercise and meditation.

Aspects of Love: On Retreat With... Laurence Freeman
Awakening: On Retreat With John Main
The Mystery Beyond: On Retreat With Bede Griffiths
Self and Environment: On Retreat With Charles Brandt
Silent Wisdom, Hidden Light: On Retreat With Eileen O'Hea